THE FAR SIDE
OF THE MOON

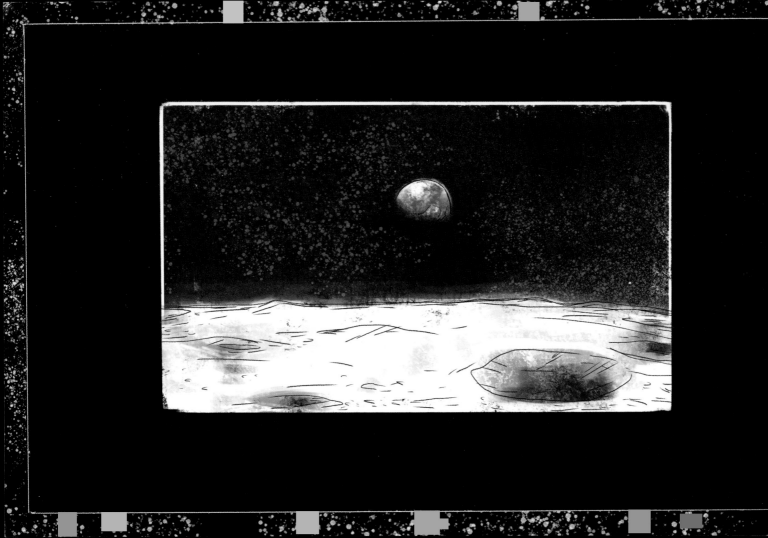

THE FAR SIDE OF THE MOON

THE STORY OF APOLLO 11's THIRD MAN

WRITTEN BY ALEX IRVINE
ILLUSTRATED BY BEN BISHOP

TILBURY HOUSE
PUBLISHERS

TO EVERYONE WHO HELPED
HUMANKIND REACH FOR THE STARS, AND
TO EVERY READER OF THIS BOOK WHO CAN REACH A
LITTLE FARTHER – BUT MOST ESPECIALLY TO MICHAEL
COLLINS, WHO HAS LIVED A LIFE THAT'S AN EXAMPLE
OF HUMBLE GREATNESS.

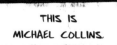

THIS IS
MICHAEL COLLINS.

HE WAS BORN ON HALLOWEEN, IN 1930.
IN ROME, ITALY, WHERE HIS FATHER WAS SERVING
IN THE ARMY. BEFORE HE TURNED 18, HE HAD
LIVED IN OKLAHOMA, TEXAS, NEW YORK, VIRGINIA,
WASHINGTON DC, AND PUERTO RICO.

HE WAS THE FIRST MAN
TO WALK IN SPACE TWICE.

HE WOULDN'T HAVE BEEN IN THE
ROTATION FOR APOLLO 11 IF HE HADN'T HAD
NECK SURGERY AND MISSED APOLLO 8.

MICHAEL COLLINS ALSO RAN THE SMITHSONIAN AIR
AND SPACE MUSEUM FOR A WHILE. BEFORE THAT HE WAS
AN ASSISTANT SECRETARY OF STATE.

HE WAS MARRIED FOR ALMOST SIXTY YEARS,
UNTIL HIS WIFE, PAT, DIED IN 2014. HE HAS
THREE CHILDREN AND SEVEN GRANDCHILDREN.

BUT THE ONLY THING MOST PEOPLE KNOW
ABOUT MICHAEL COLLINS IS THAT HE DIDN'T
GET TO WALK ON THE MOON.

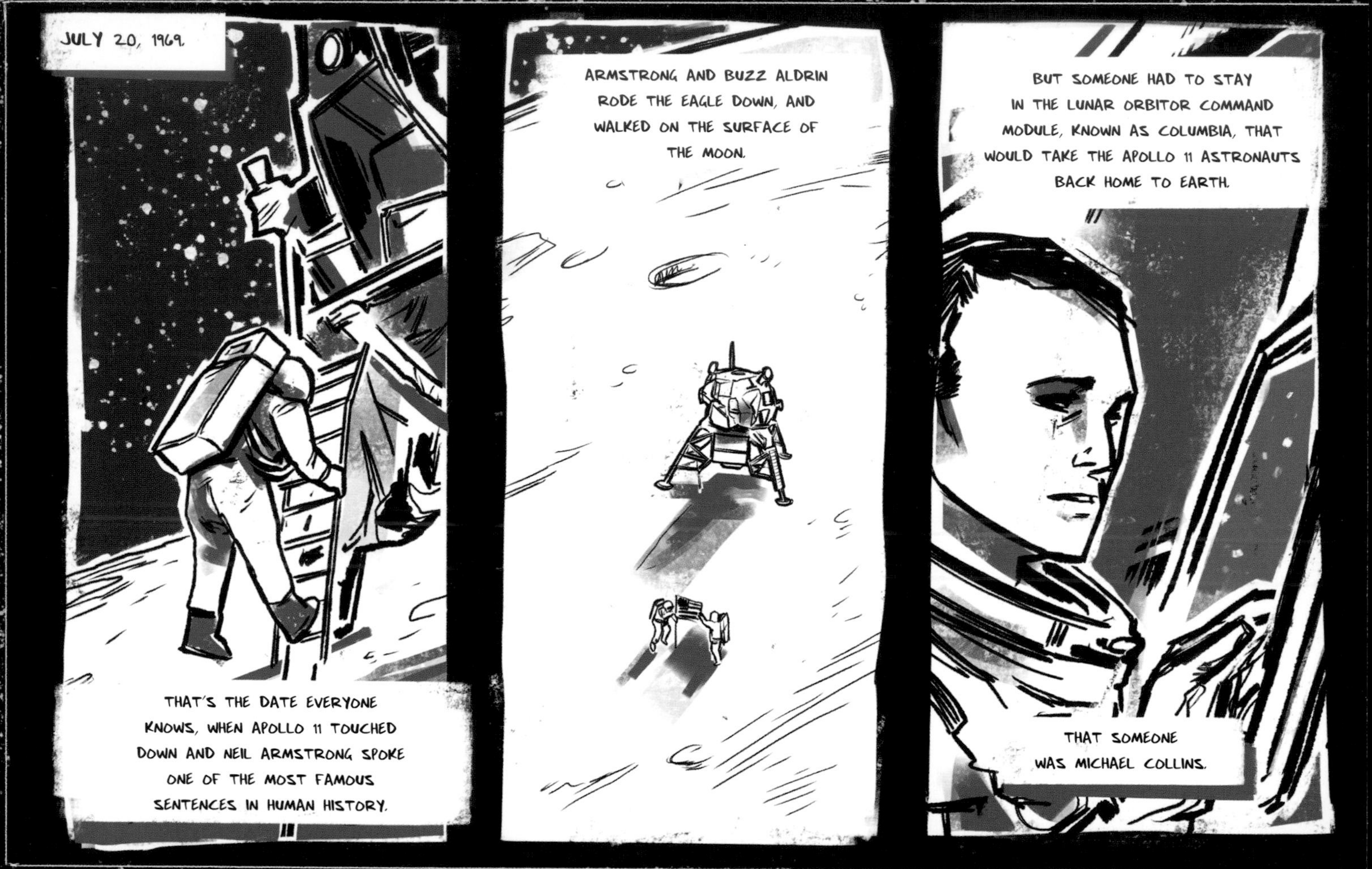
JULY 20, 1969.
THAT'S THE DATE EVERYONE KNOWS, WHEN APOLLO 11 TOUCHED DOWN AND NEIL ARMSTRONG SPOKE ONE OF THE MOST FAMOUS SENTENCES IN HUMAN HISTORY.
ARMSTRONG AND BUZZ ALDRIN RODE THE EAGLE DOWN, AND WALKED ON THE SURFACE OF THE MOON.
BUT SOMEONE HAD TO STAY IN THE LUNAR ORBITOR COMMAND MODULE, KNOWN AS COLUMBIA, THAT WOULD TAKE THE APOLLO 11 ASTRONAUTS BACK HOME TO EARTH.
THAT SOMEONE WAS MICHAEL COLLINS.

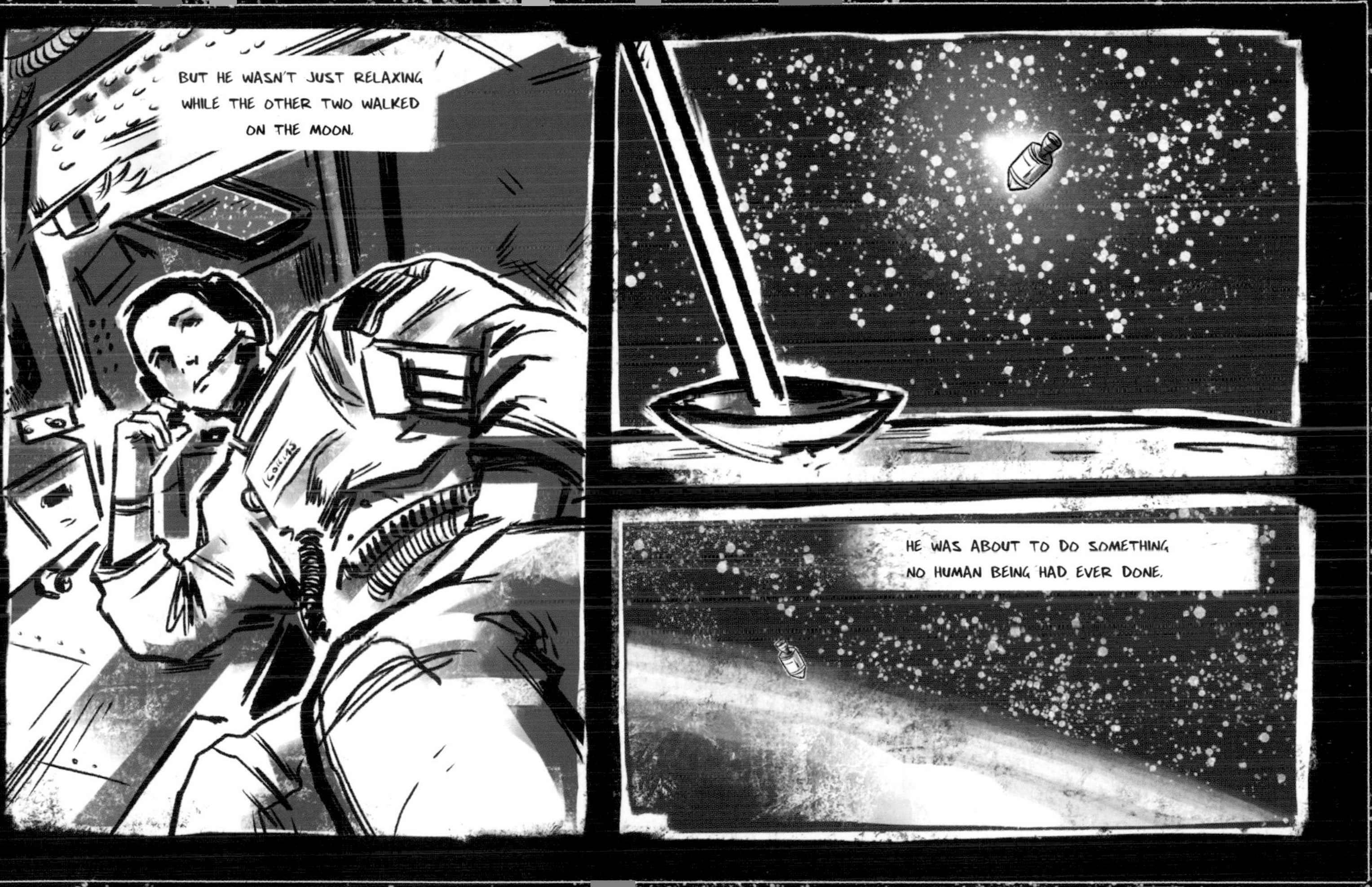
BUT HE WASN'T JUST RELAXING WHILE THE OTHER TWO WALKED ON THE MOON.
HE WAS ABOUT TO DO SOMETHING NO HUMAN BEING HAD EVER DONE.

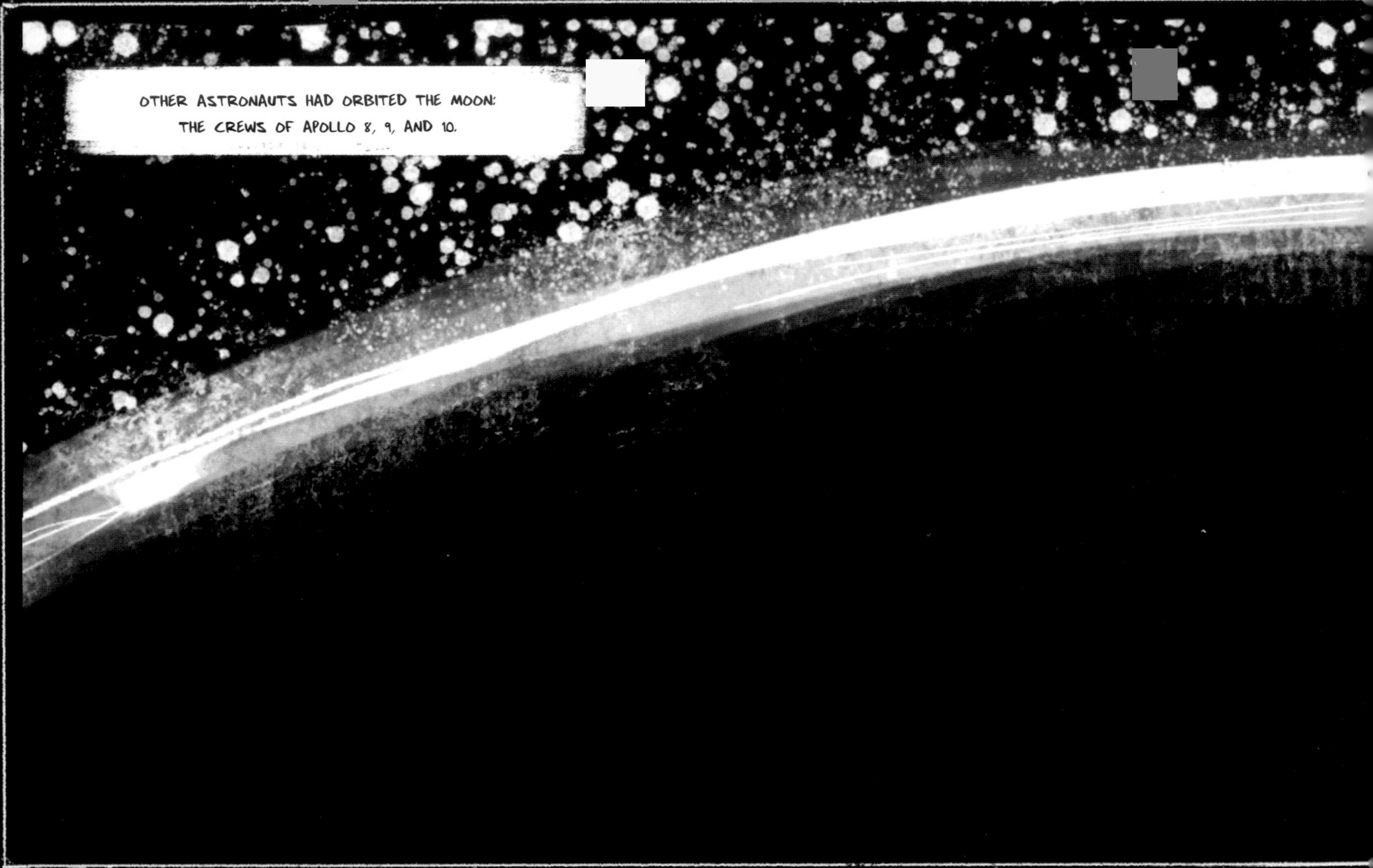
OTHER ASTRONAUTS HAD ORBITED THE MOON: THE CREWS OF APOLLO 8, 9, AND 10.

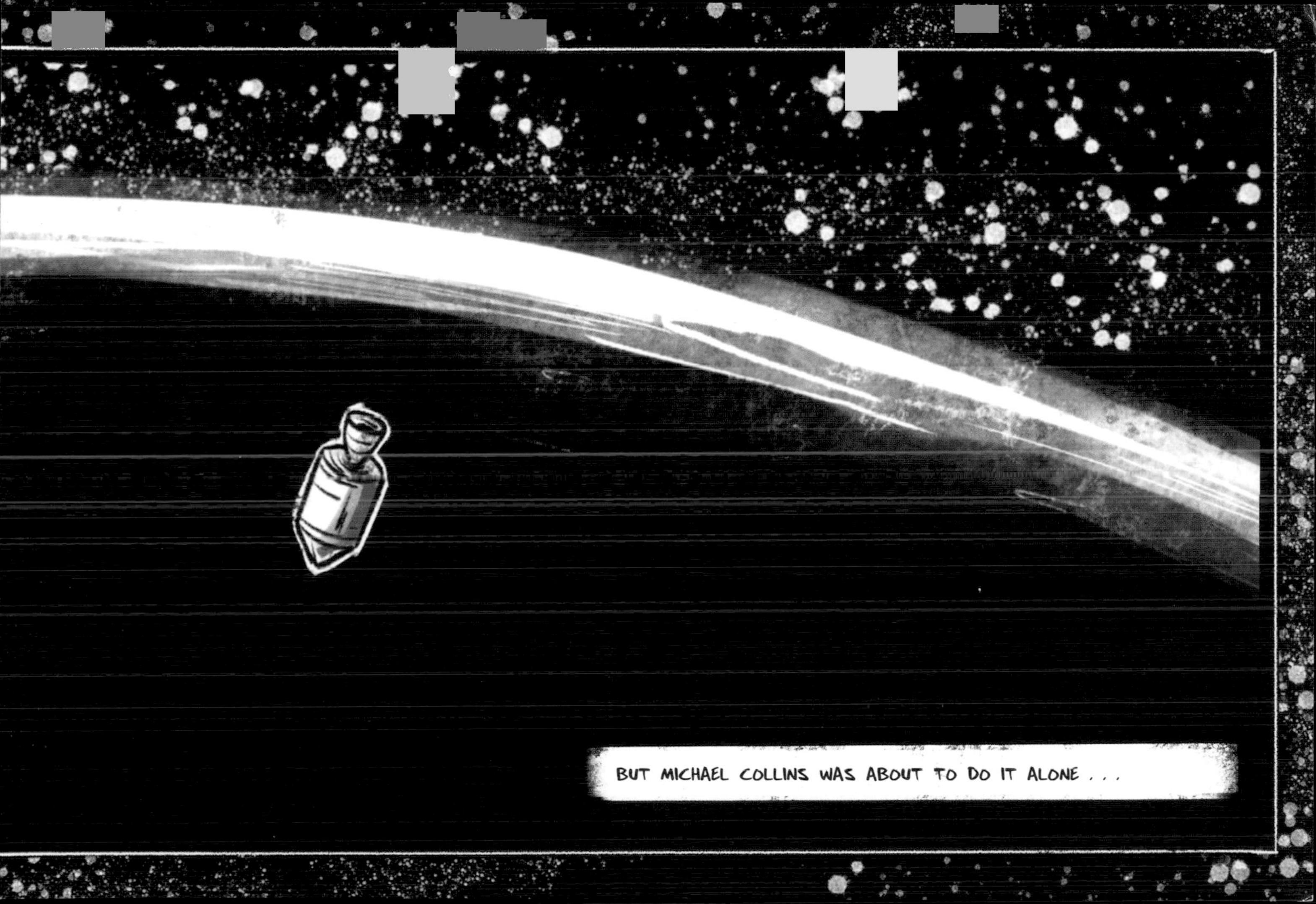
BUT MICHAEL COLLINS WAS ABOUT TO DO IT ALONE . . .

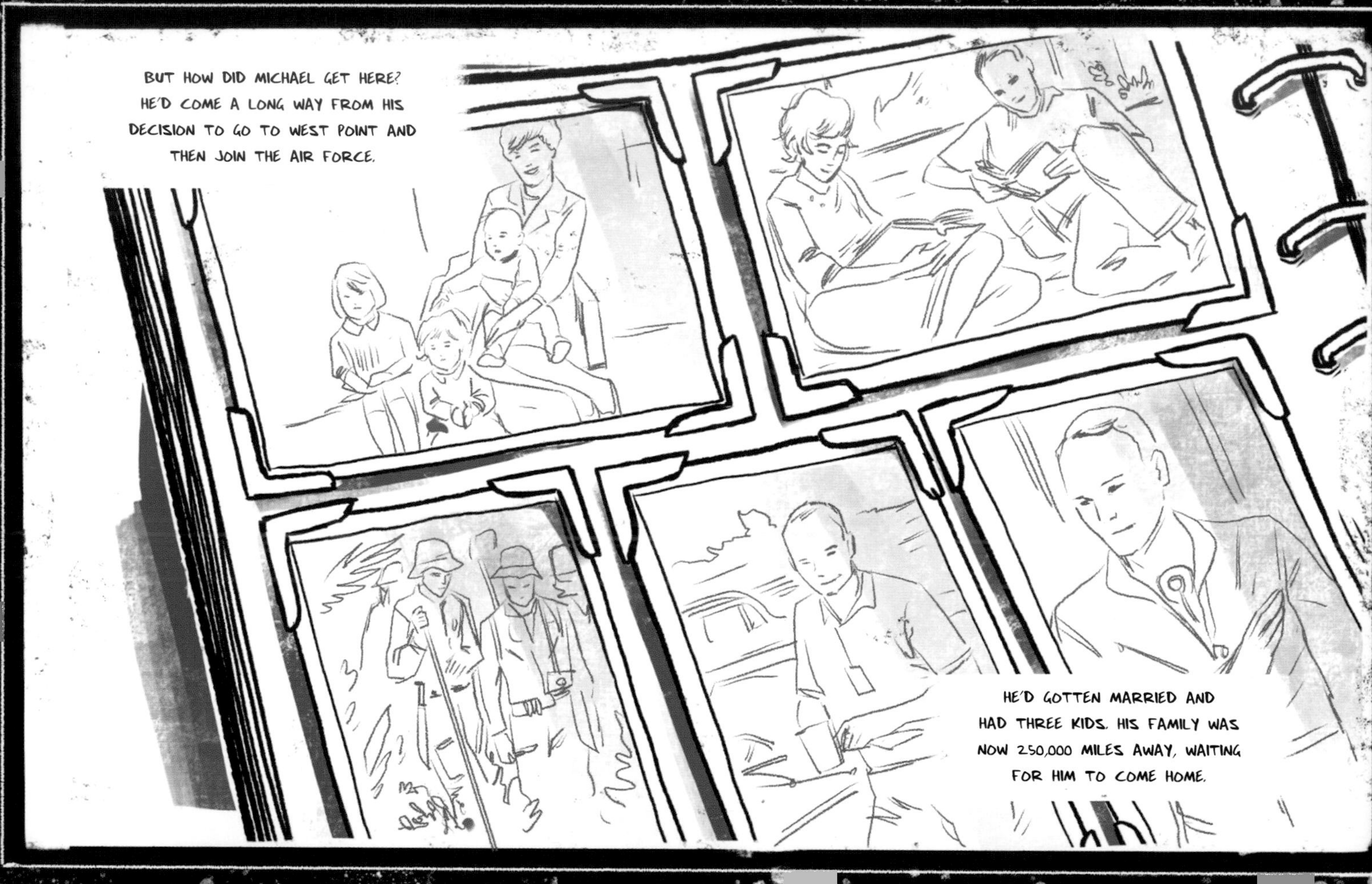
BUT HOW DID MICHAEL GET HERE? HE'D COME A LONG WAY FROM HIS DECISION TO GO TO WEST POINT AND THEN JOIN THE AIR FORCE.
HE'D GOTTEN MARRIED AND HAD THREE KIDS. HIS FAMILY WAS NOW 250,000 MILES AWAY, WAITING FOR HIM TO COME HOME.

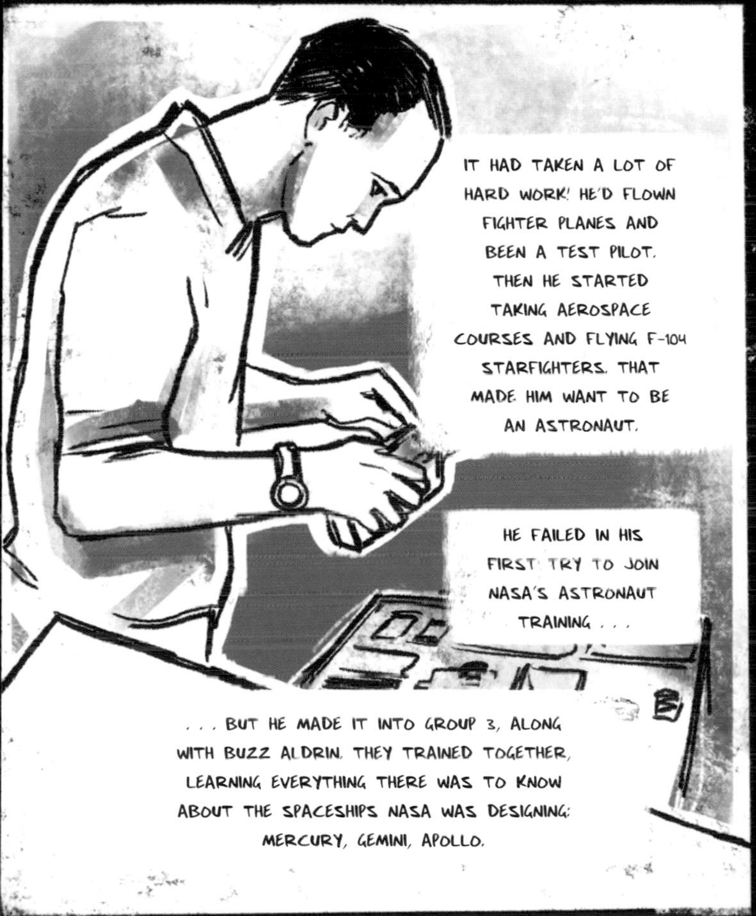
IT HAD TAKEN A LOT OF HARD WORK! HE'D FLOWN FIGHTER PLANES AND BEEN A TEST PILOT. THEN HE STARTED TAKING AEROSPACE COURSES AND FLYING F-104 STARFIGHTERS. THAT MADE HIM WANT TO BE AN ASTRONAUT.
HE FAILED IN HIS FIRST TRY TO JOIN NASA'S ASTRONAUT TRAINING . . .
. . . BUT HE MADE IT INTO GROUP 3, ALONG WITH BUZZ ALDRIN. THEY TRAINED TOGETHER, LEARNING EVERYTHING THERE WAS TO KNOW ABOUT THE SPACESHIPS NASA WAS DESIGNING: MERCURY, GEMINI, APOLLO.

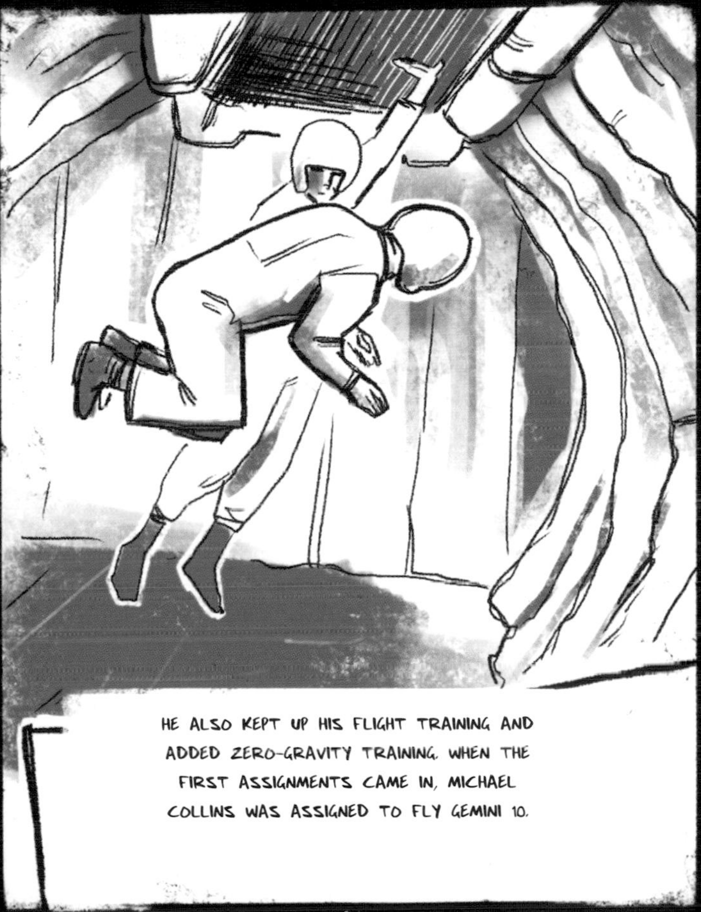
HE ALSO KEPT UP HIS FLIGHT TRAINING AND ADDED ZERO-GRAVITY TRAINING. WHEN THE FIRST ASSIGNMENTS CAME IN, MICHAEL COLLINS WAS ASSIGNED TO FLY GEMINI 10.

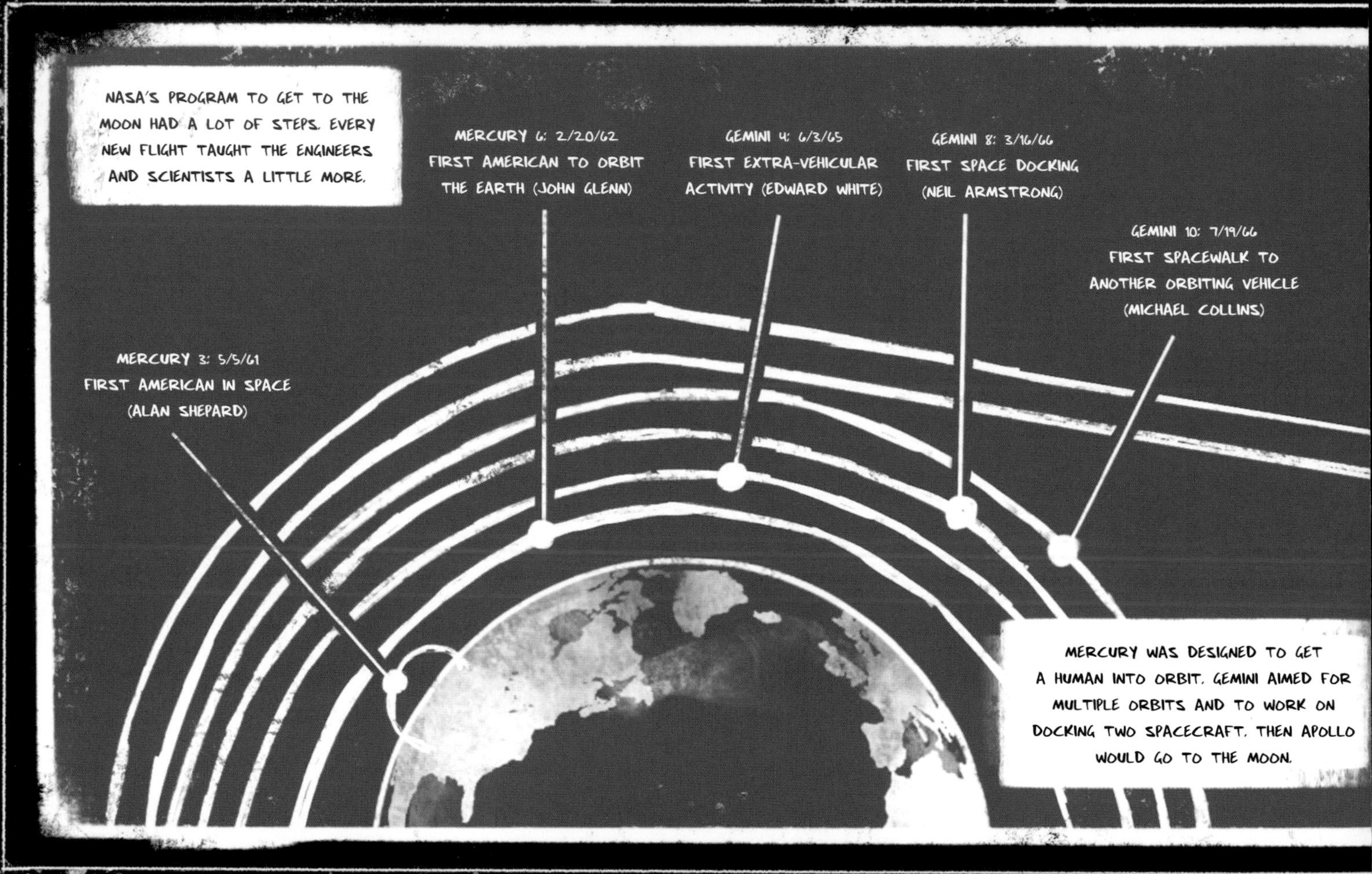
NASA'S PROGRAM TO GET TO THE MOON HAD A LOT OF STEPS. EVERY NEW FLIGHT TAUGHT THE ENGINEERS AND SCIENTISTS A LITTLE MORE.
MERCURY 6: 2/20/62
FIRST AMERICAN TO ORBIT THE EARTH (JOHN GLENN)
GEMINI 4: 6/3/65
FIRST EXTRA-VEHICULAR ACTIVITY (EDWARD WHITE)
GEMINI 8: 3/16/66
FIRST SPACE DOCKING (NEIL ARMSTRONG)
GEMINI 10: 7/19/66
FIRST SPACEWALK TO ANOTHER ORBITING VEHICLE (MICHAEL COLLINS)
MERCURY 3: 5/5/61
FIRST AMERICAN IN SPACE (ALAN SHEPARD)
MERCURY WAS DESIGNED TO GET A HUMAN INTO ORBIT. GEMINI AIMED FOR MULTIPLE ORBITS AND TO WORK ON DOCKING TWO SPACECRAFT. THEN APOLLO WOULD GO TO THE MOON.

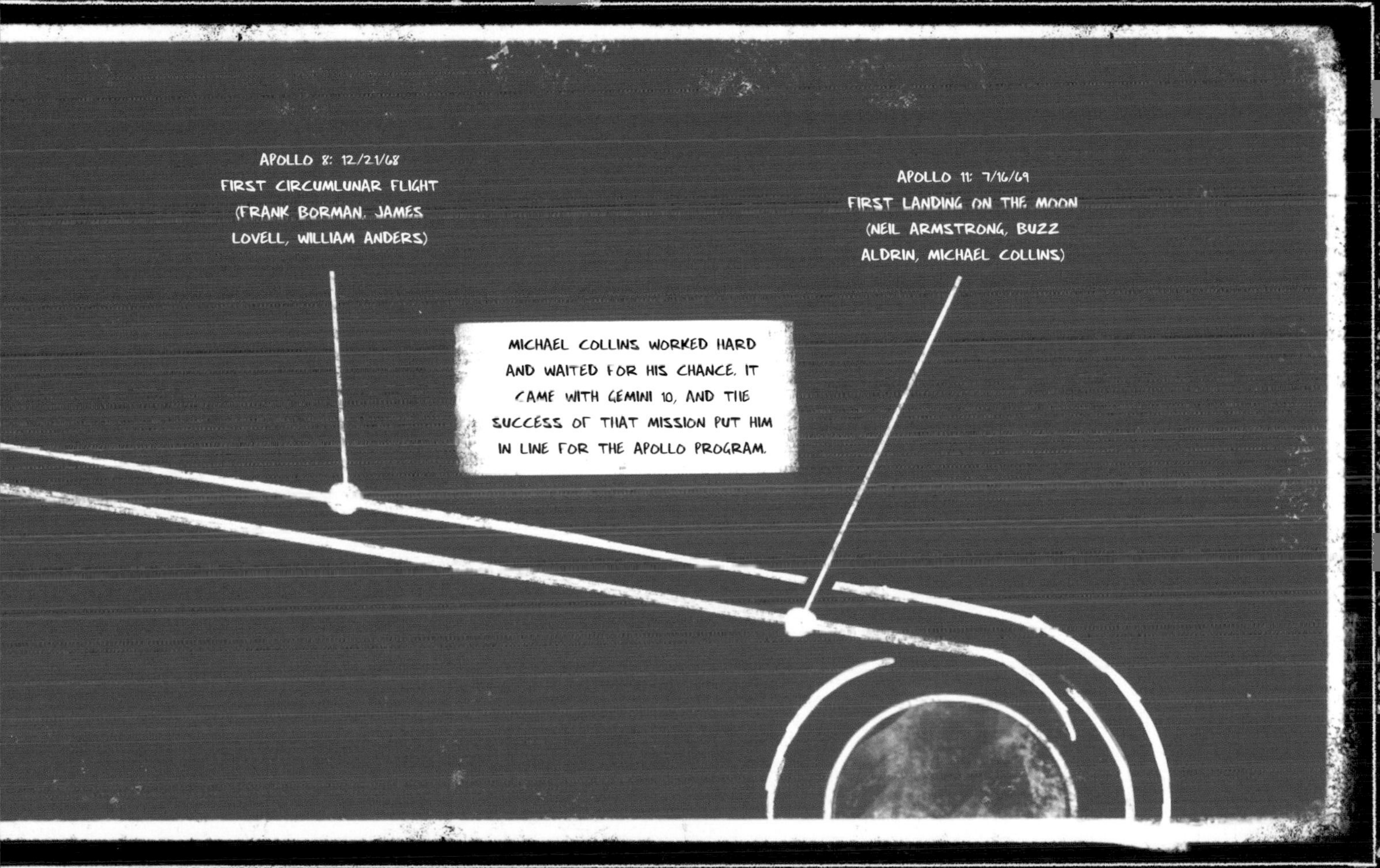
APOLLO 8: 12/21/68
FIRST CIRCUMLUNAR FLIGHT
(FRANK BORMAN, JAMES
LOVELL, WILLIAM ANDERS)
MICHAEL COLLINS WORKED HARD AND WAITED FOR HIS CHANCE. IT CAME WITH GEMINI 10, AND THE SUCCESS OF THAT MISSION PUT HIM IN LINE FOR THE APOLLO PROGRAM.
APOLLO 11: 7/16/69
FIRST LANDING ON THE MOON
(NEIL ARMSTRONG, BUZZ
ALDRIN, MICHAEL COLLINS)

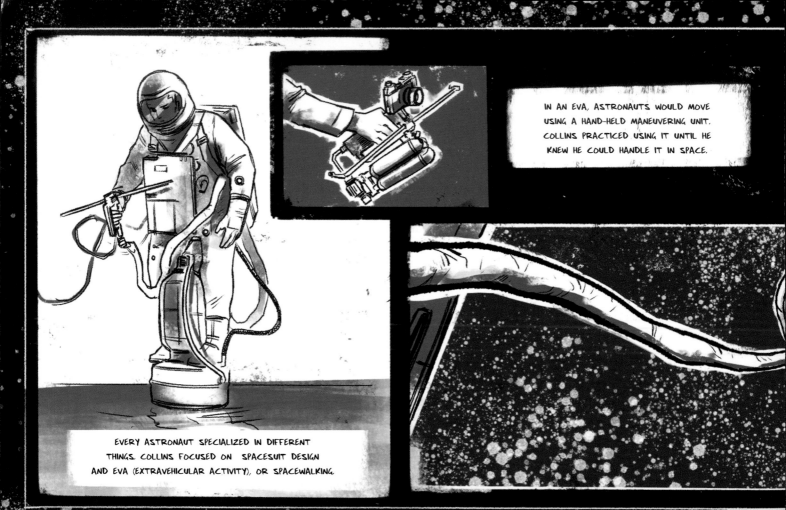

IN AN EVA, ASTRONAUTS WOULD MOVE USING A HAND-HELD MANEUVERING UNIT. COLLINS PRACTICED USING IT UNTIL HE KNEW HE COULD HANDLE IT IN SPACE.

EVERY ASTRONAUT SPECIALIZED IN DIFFERENT THINGS. COLLINS FOCUSED ON SPACESUIT DESIGN AND EVA (EXTRAVEHICULAR ACTIVITY), OR SPACEWALKING.

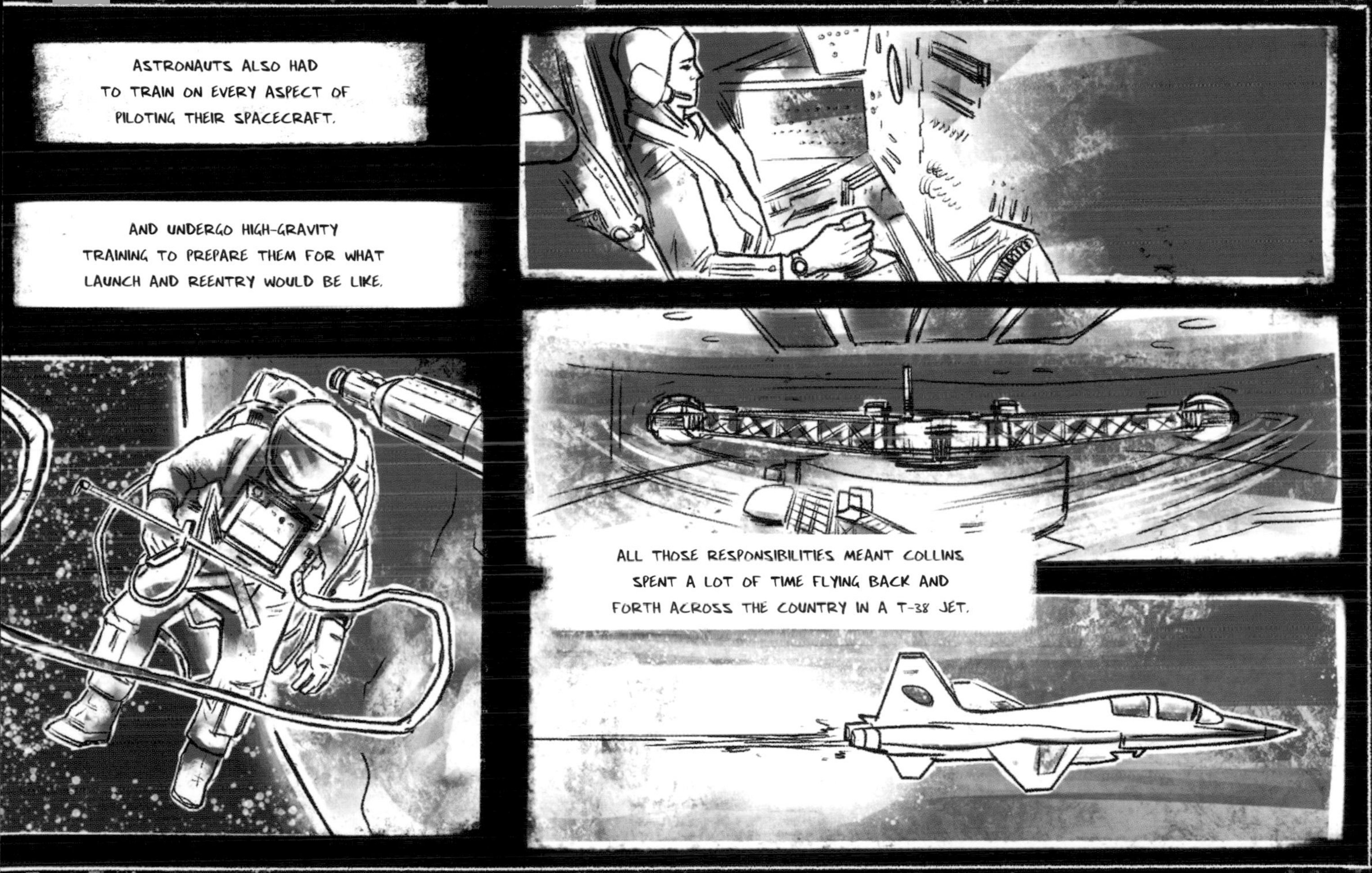
ASTRONAUTS ALSO HAD TO TRAIN ON EVERY ASPECT OF PILOTING THEIR SPACECRAFT.
AND UNDERGO HIGH-GRAVITY TRAINING TO PREPARE THEM FOR WHAT LAUNCH AND REENTRY WOULD BE LIKE.
ALL THOSE RESPONSIBILITIES MEANT COLLINS SPENT A LOT OF TIME FLYING BACK AND FORTH ACROSS THE COUNTRY IN A T-38 JET.

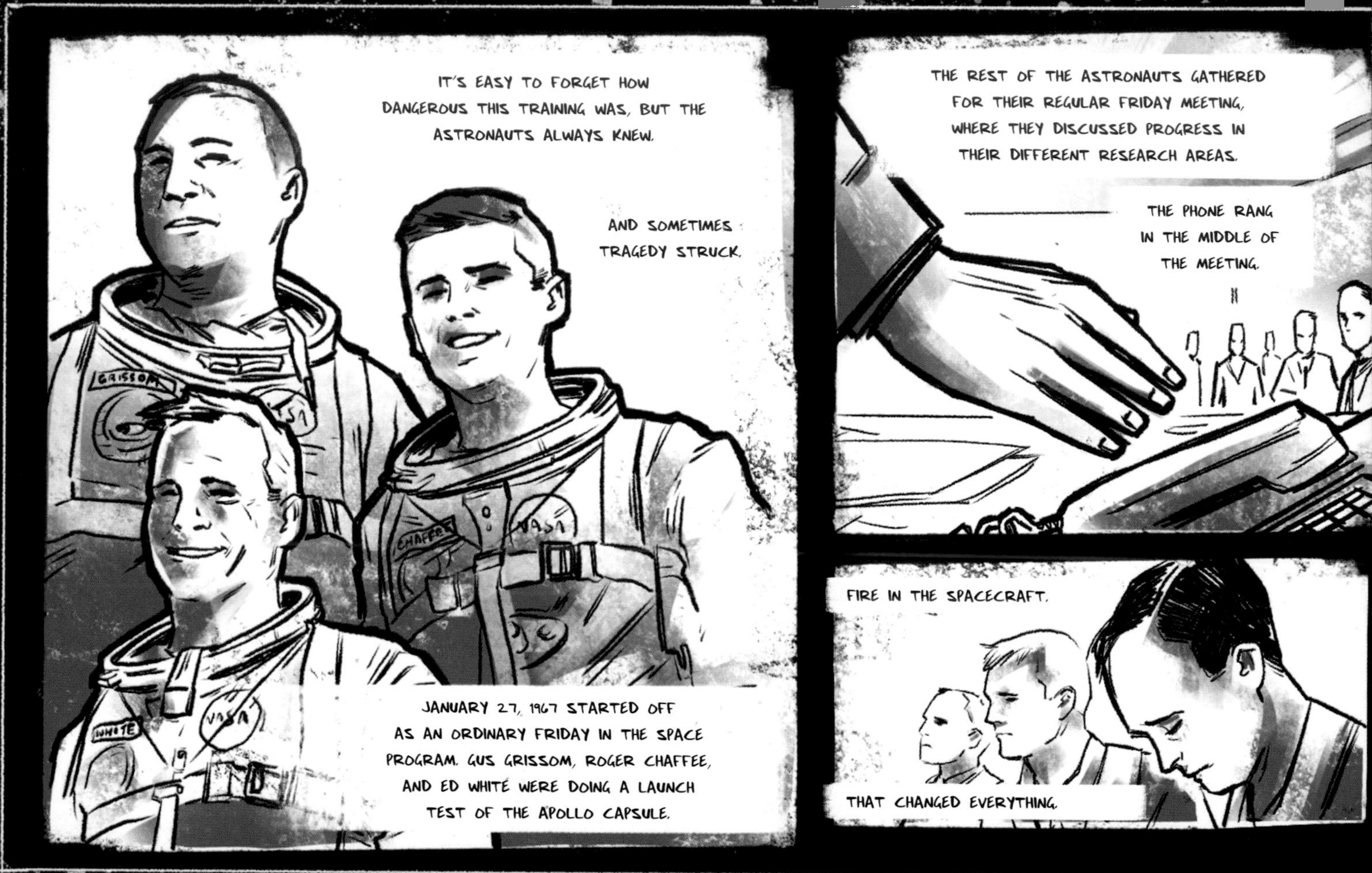
IT'S EASY TO FORGET HOW DANGEROUS THIS TRAINING WAS, BUT THE ASTRONAUTS ALWAYS KNEW.
AND SOMETIMES TRAGEDY STRUCK.
JANUARY 27, 1967 STARTED OFF AS AN ORDINARY FRIDAY IN THE SPACE PROGRAM. GUS GRISSOM, ROGER CHAFFEE, AND ED WHITE WERE DOING A LAUNCH TEST OF THE APOLLO CAPSULE.
THE REST OF THE ASTRONAUTS GATHERED FOR THEIR REGULAR FRIDAY MEETING, WHERE THEY DISCUSSED PROGRESS IN THEIR DIFFERENT RESEARCH AREAS.
THE PHONE RANG IN THE MIDDLE OF THE MEETING.
FIRE IN THE SPACECRAFT.
THAT CHANGED EVERYTHING.

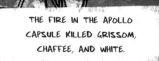

THE FIRE IN THE APOLLO CAPSULE KILLED GRISSOM, CHAFFEE, AND WHITE.

IT ALSO SET THE APOLLO PROGRAM BACK MORE THAN A YEAR. NASA INVESTIGATED THE CAUSE OF THE FIRE AND INSTITUTED NEW SAFETY PROTOCOLS SO NOTHING LIKE THIS WOULD EVER HAPPEN AGAIN.

THE SURVIVING ASTRONAUTS ALSO HELPED THE FAMILIES OF GRISSOM, CHAFFEE, AND WHITE. THEY KNEW IT COULD HAVE BEEN ANY OF THEM IN THAT CAPSULE.

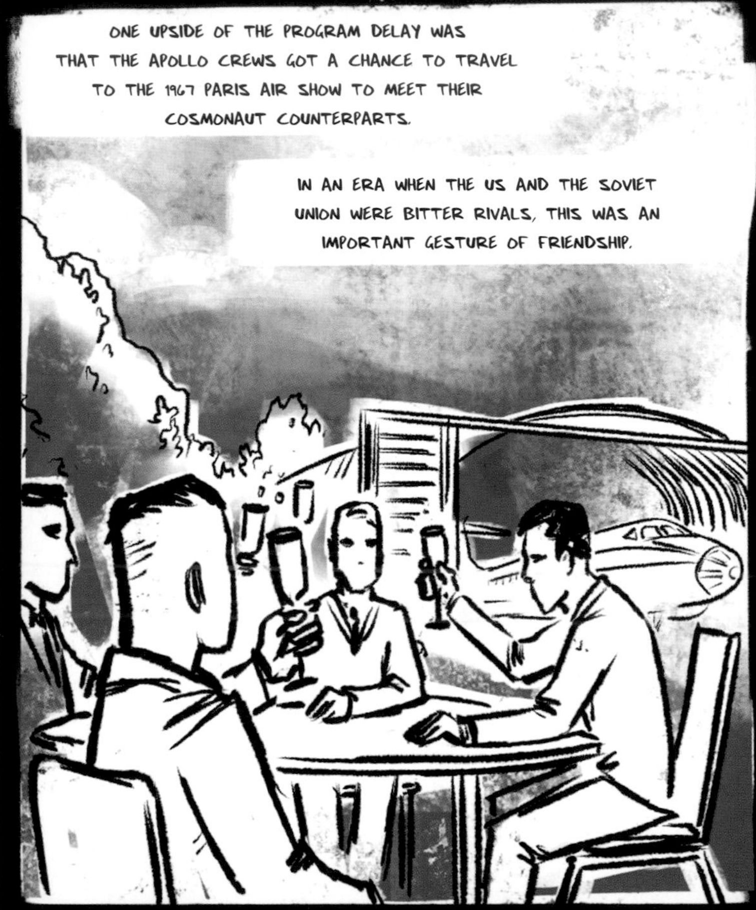
ONE UPSIDE OF THE PROGRAM DELAY WAS THAT THE APOLLO CREWS GOT A CHANCE TO TRAVEL TO THE 1967 PARIS AIR SHOW TO MEET THEIR COSMONAUT COUNTERPARTS.
IN AN ERA WHEN THE US AND THE SOVIET UNION WERE BITTER RIVALS, THIS WAS AN IMPORTANT GESTURE OF FRIENDSHIP.

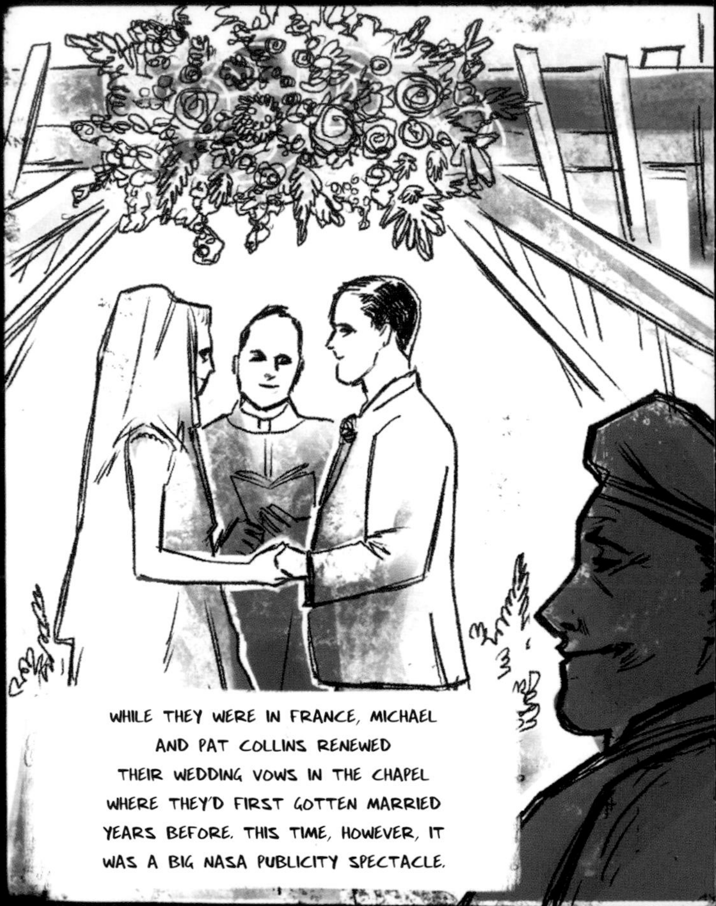
WHILE THEY WERE IN FRANCE, MICHAEL AND PAT COLLINS RENEWED THEIR WEDDING VOWS IN THE CHAPEL WHERE THEY'D FIRST GOTTEN MARRIED YEARS BEFORE. THIS TIME, HOWEVER, IT WAS A BIG NASA PUBLICITY SPECTACLE.

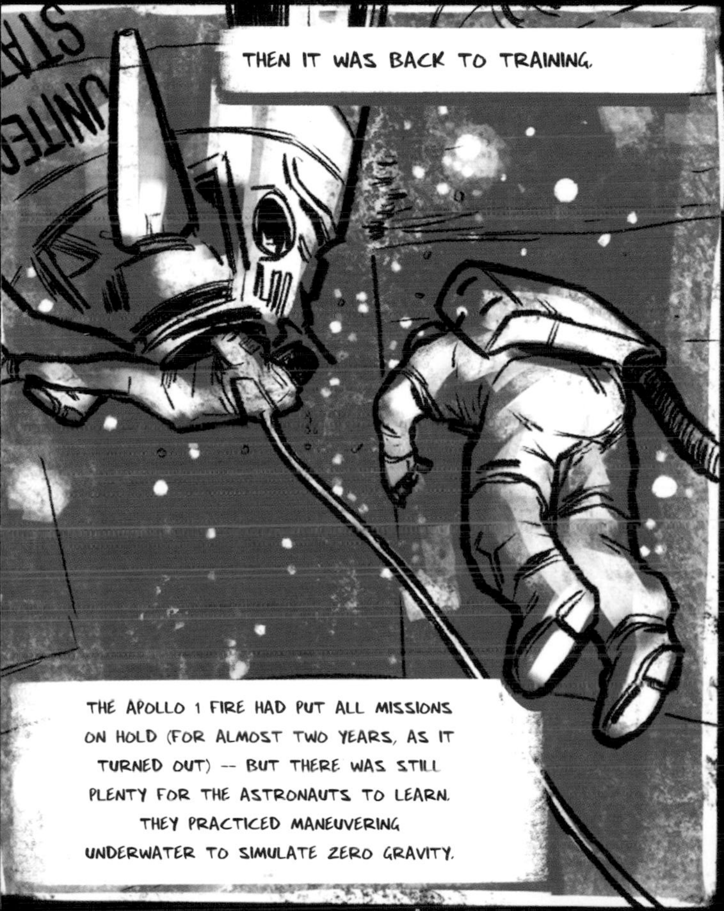
THEN IT WAS BACK TO TRAINING.
THE APOLLO 1 FIRE HAD PUT ALL MISSIONS ON HOLD (FOR ALMOST TWO YEARS, AS IT TURNED OUT) -- BUT THERE WAS STILL PLENTY FOR THE ASTRONAUTS TO LEARN. THEY PRACTICED MANEUVERING UNDERWATER TO SIMULATE ZERO GRAVITY.

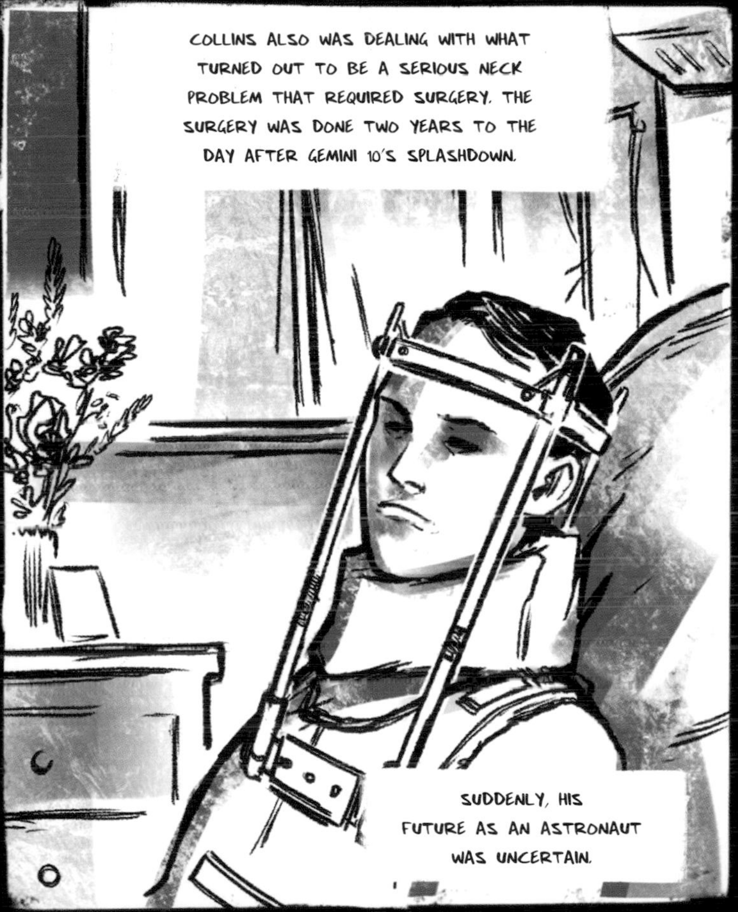
COLLINS ALSO WAS DEALING WITH WHAT TURNED OUT TO BE A SERIOUS NECK PROBLEM THAT REQUIRED SURGERY. THE SURGERY WAS DONE TWO YEARS TO THE DAY AFTER GEMINI 10'S SPLASHDOWN.
SUDDENLY, HIS FUTURE AS AN ASTRONAUT WAS UNCERTAIN.

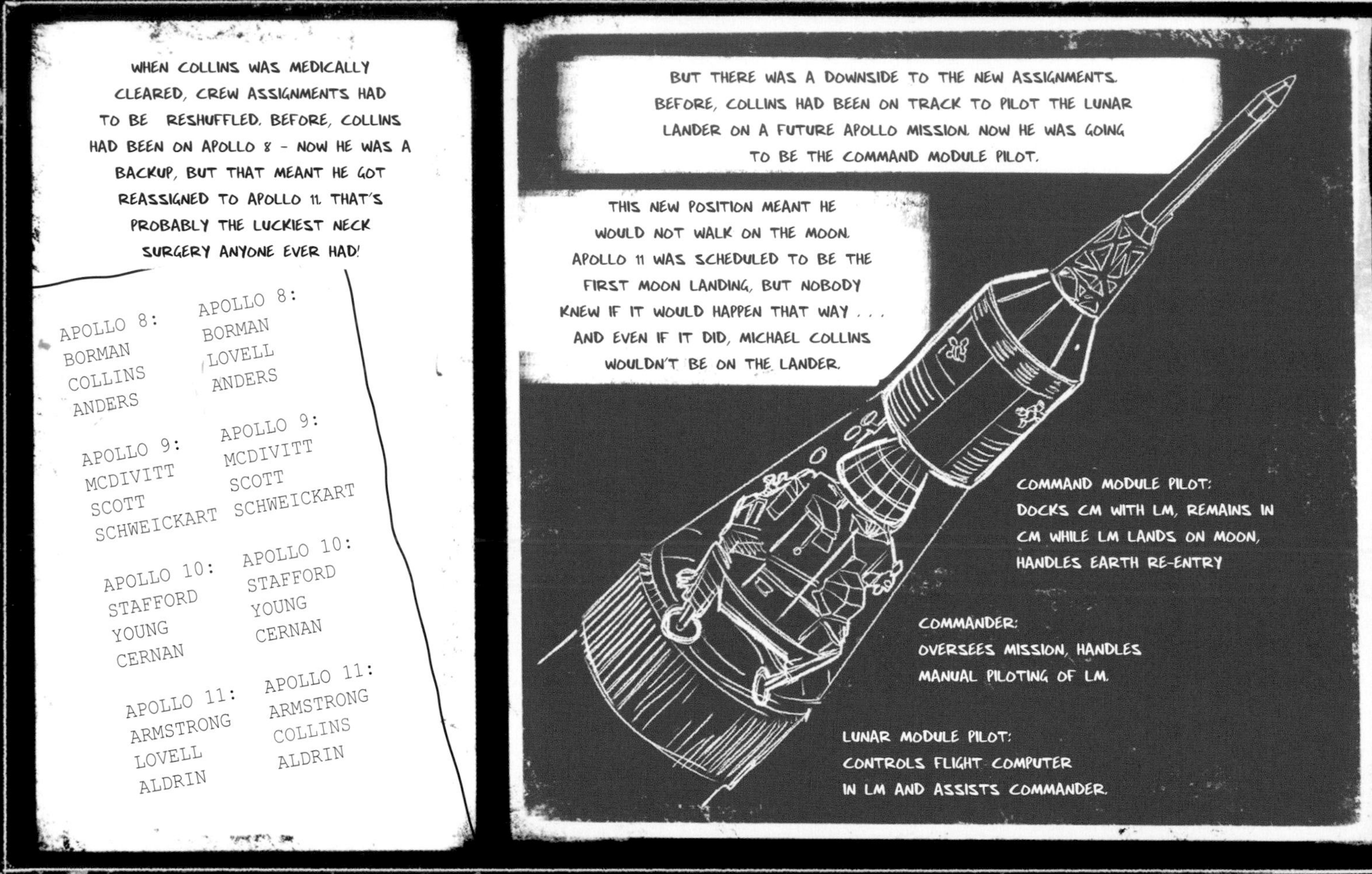
WHEN COLLINS WAS MEDICALLY CLEARED, CREW ASSIGNMENTS HAD TO BE RESHUFFLED. BEFORE, COLLINS HAD BEEN ON APOLLO 8 – NOW HE WAS A BACKUP, BUT THAT MEANT HE GOT REASSIGNED TO APOLLO 11. THAT'S PROBABLY THE LUCKIEST NECK SURGERY ANYONE EVER HAD!
APOLLO 8: BORMAN COLLINS ANDERS
APOLLO 9: MCDIVITT SCOTT SCHWEICKART
APOLLO 10: STAFFORD YOUNG CERNAN
APOLLO 11: ARMSTRONG LOVELL ALDRIN
APOLLO 8: BORMAN LOVELL ANDERS
APOLLO 9: MCDIVITT SCOTT SCHWEICKART
APOLLO 10: STAFFORD YOUNG CERNAN
APOLLO 11: ARMSTRONG COLLINS ALDRIN
BUT THERE WAS A DOWNSIDE TO THE NEW ASSIGNMENTS. BEFORE, COLLINS HAD BEEN ON TRACK TO PILOT THE LUNAR LANDER ON A FUTURE APOLLO MISSION. NOW HE WAS GOING TO BE THE COMMAND MODULE PILOT.
THIS NEW POSITION MEANT HE WOULD NOT WALK ON THE MOON. APOLLO 11 WAS SCHEDULED TO BE THE FIRST MOON LANDING, BUT NOBODY KNEW IF IT WOULD HAPPEN THAT WAY . . . AND EVEN IF IT DID, MICHAEL COLLINS WOULDN'T BE ON THE LANDER.
COMMAND MODULE PILOT: DOCKS CM WITH LM, REMAINS IN CM WHILE LM LANDS ON MOON, HANDLES EARTH RE-ENTRY
COMMANDER: OVERSEES MISSION, HANDLES MANUAL PILOTING OF LM.
LUNAR MODULE PILOT: CONTROLS FLIGHT COMPUTER IN LM AND ASSISTS COMMANDER.

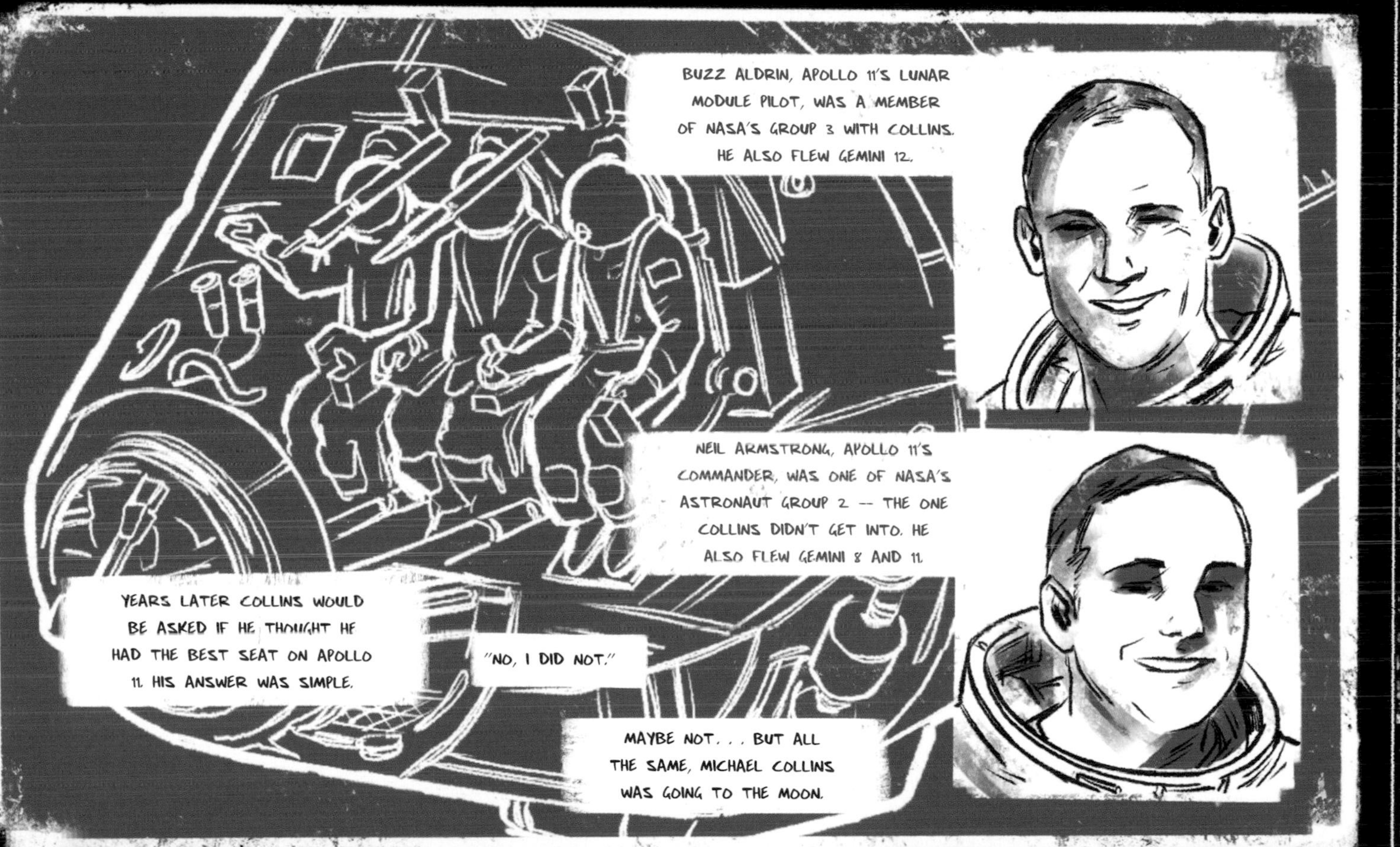
BUZZ ALDRIN, APOLLO 11'S LUNAR MODULE PILOT, WAS A MEMBER OF NASA'S GROUP 3 WITH COLLINS. HE ALSO FLEW GEMINI 12.
NEIL ARMSTRONG, APOLLO 11'S COMMANDER, WAS ONE OF NASA'S ASTRONAUT GROUP 2 -- THE ONE COLLINS DIDN'T GET INTO. HE ALSO FLEW GEMINI 8 AND 11.
YEARS LATER COLLINS WOULD BE ASKED IF HE THOUGHT HE HAD THE BEST SEAT ON APOLLO 11. HIS ANSWER WAS SIMPLE.
"NO, I DID NOT."
MAYBE NOT. . . BUT ALL THE SAME, MICHAEL COLLINS WAS GOING TO THE MOON.

WHILE THE ASTRONAUTS TRAINED, COLLINS' WORK ON SPACESUIT DESIGN WAS CRITICAL. SPACESUITS HAD TO KEEP ASTRONAUTS SAFE WHILE ALSO BEING FLEXIBLE ENOUGH TO LET THEM WORK IN LOW OR ZERO GRAVITY. AFTER YEARS OF WORK, COLLINS AND THE DESIGN TEAM CAME UP WITH THE APOLLO SUIT.

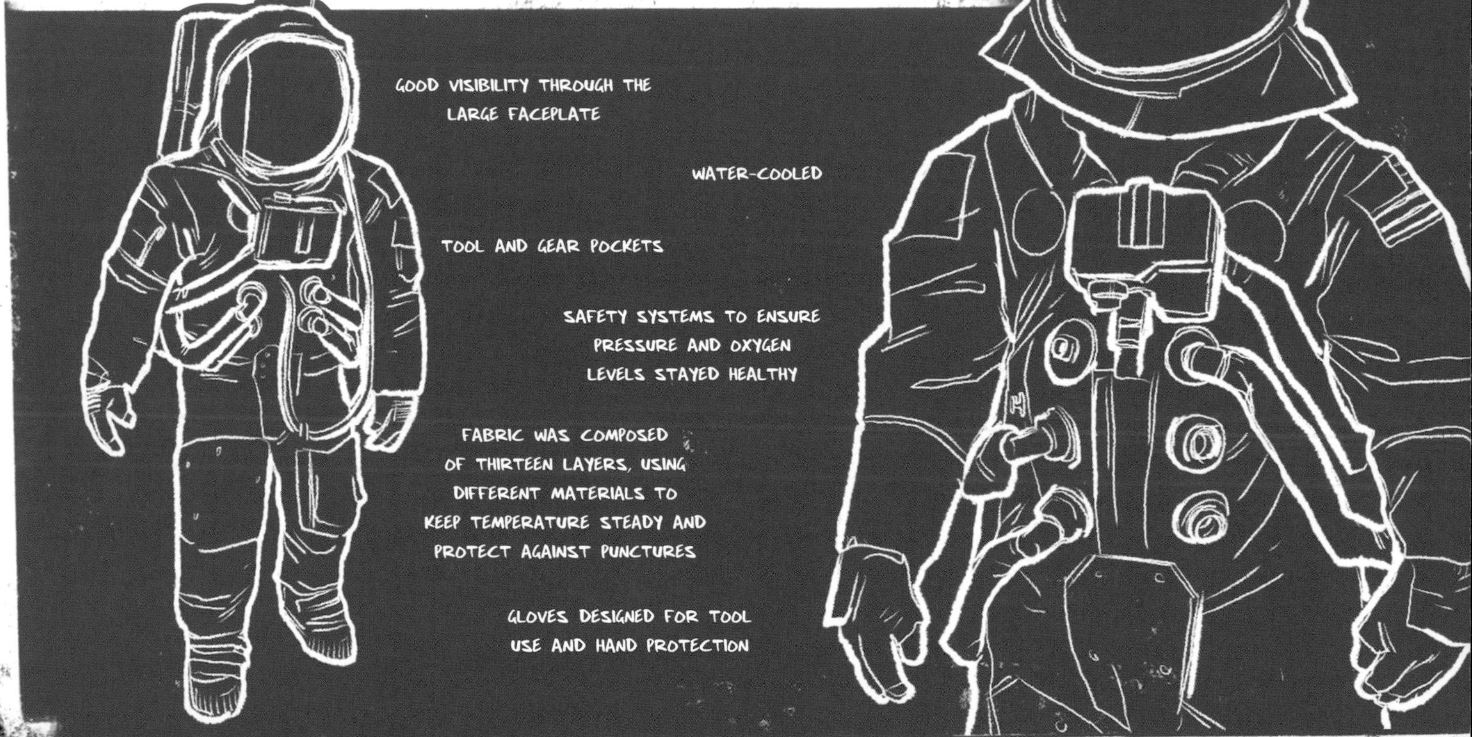
GOOD VISIBILITY THROUGH THE LARGE FACEPLATE
WATER-COOLED
TOOL AND GEAR POCKETS
SAFETY SYSTEMS TO ENSURE PRESSURE AND OXYGEN LEVELS STAYED HEALTHY
FABRIC WAS COMPOSED OF THIRTEEN LAYERS, USING DIFFERENT MATERIALS TO KEEP TEMPERATURE STEADY AND PROTECT AGAINST PUNCTURES
GLOVES DESIGNED FOR TOOL USE AND HAND PROTECTION

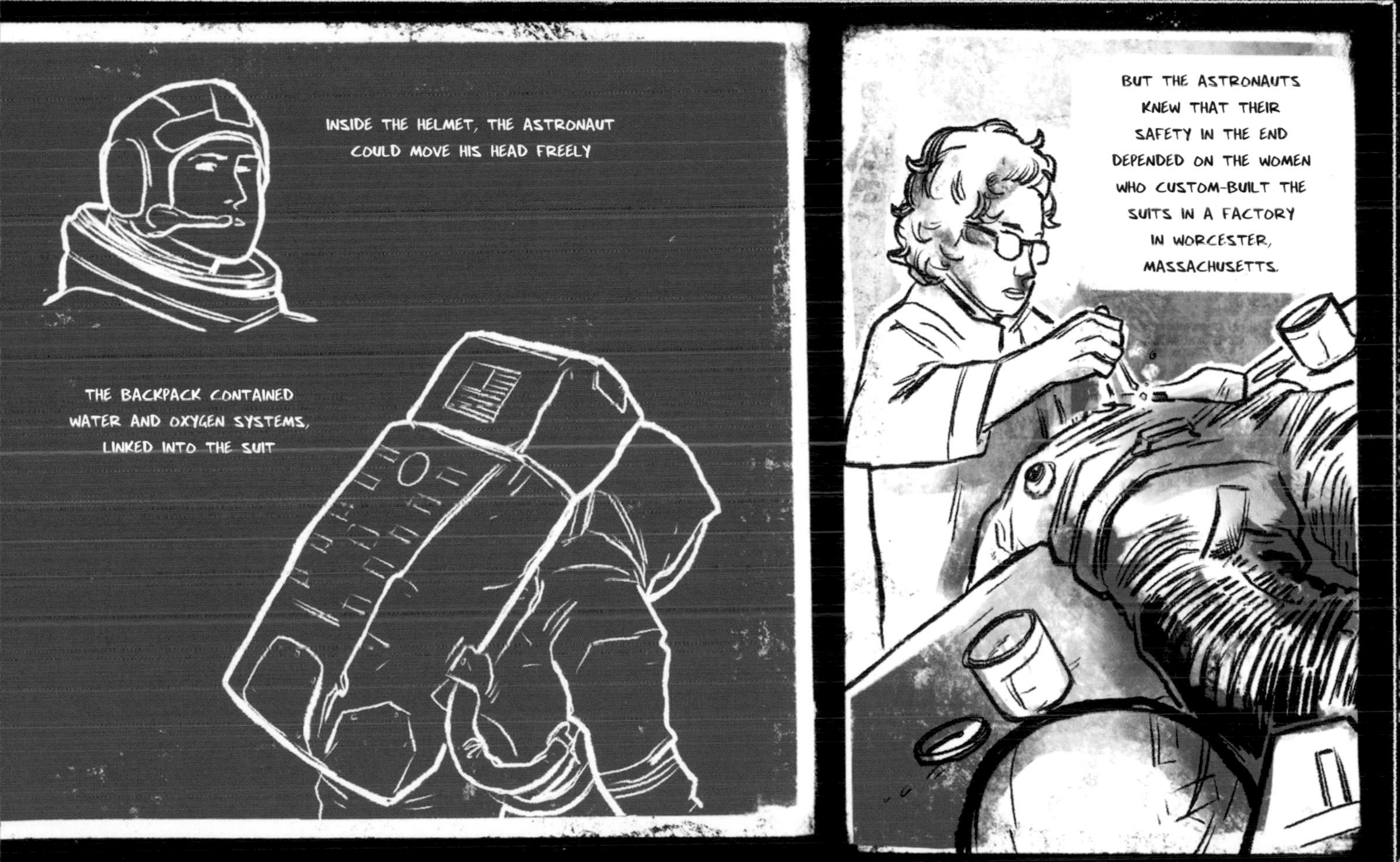
INSIDE THE HELMET, THE ASTRONAUT COULD MOVE HIS HEAD FREELY
THE BACKPACK CONTAINED WATER AND OXYGEN SYSTEMS, LINKED INTO THE SUIT
BUT THE ASTRONAUTS KNEW THAT THEIR SAFETY IN THE END DEPENDED ON THE WOMEN WHO CUSTOM-BUILT THE SUITS IN A FACTORY IN WORCESTER, MASSACHUSETTS.

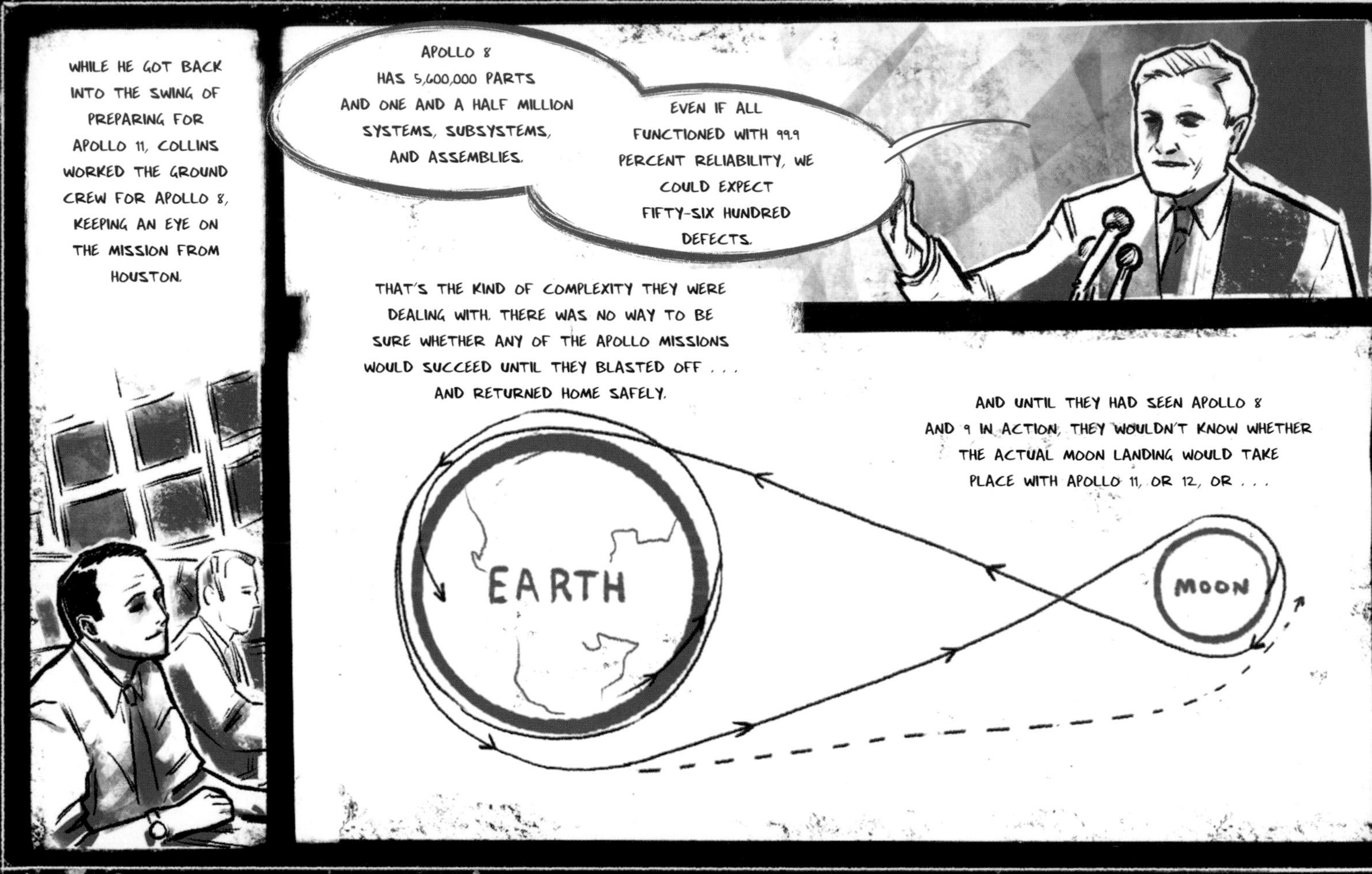
WHILE HE GOT BACK INTO THE SWING OF PREPARING FOR APOLLO 11, COLLINS WORKED THE GROUND CREW FOR APOLLO 8, KEEPING AN EYE ON THE MISSION FROM HOUSTON.
APOLLO 8 HAS 5,600,000 PARTS AND ONE AND A HALF MILLION SYSTEMS, SUBSYSTEMS, AND ASSEMBLIES.
EVEN IF ALL FUNCTIONED WITH 99.9 PERCENT RELIABILITY, WE COULD EXPECT FIFTY-SIX HUNDRED DEFECTS.
THAT'S THE KIND OF COMPLEXITY THEY WERE DEALING WITH. THERE WAS NO WAY TO BE SURE WHETHER ANY OF THE APOLLO MISSIONS WOULD SUCCEED UNTIL THEY BLASTED OFF . . . AND RETURNED HOME SAFELY.
AND UNTIL THEY HAD SEEN APOLLO 8 AND 9 IN ACTION, THEY WOULDN'T KNOW WHETHER THE ACTUAL MOON LANDING WOULD TAKE PLACE WITH APOLLO 11, OR 12, OR . . .
EARTH
MOON

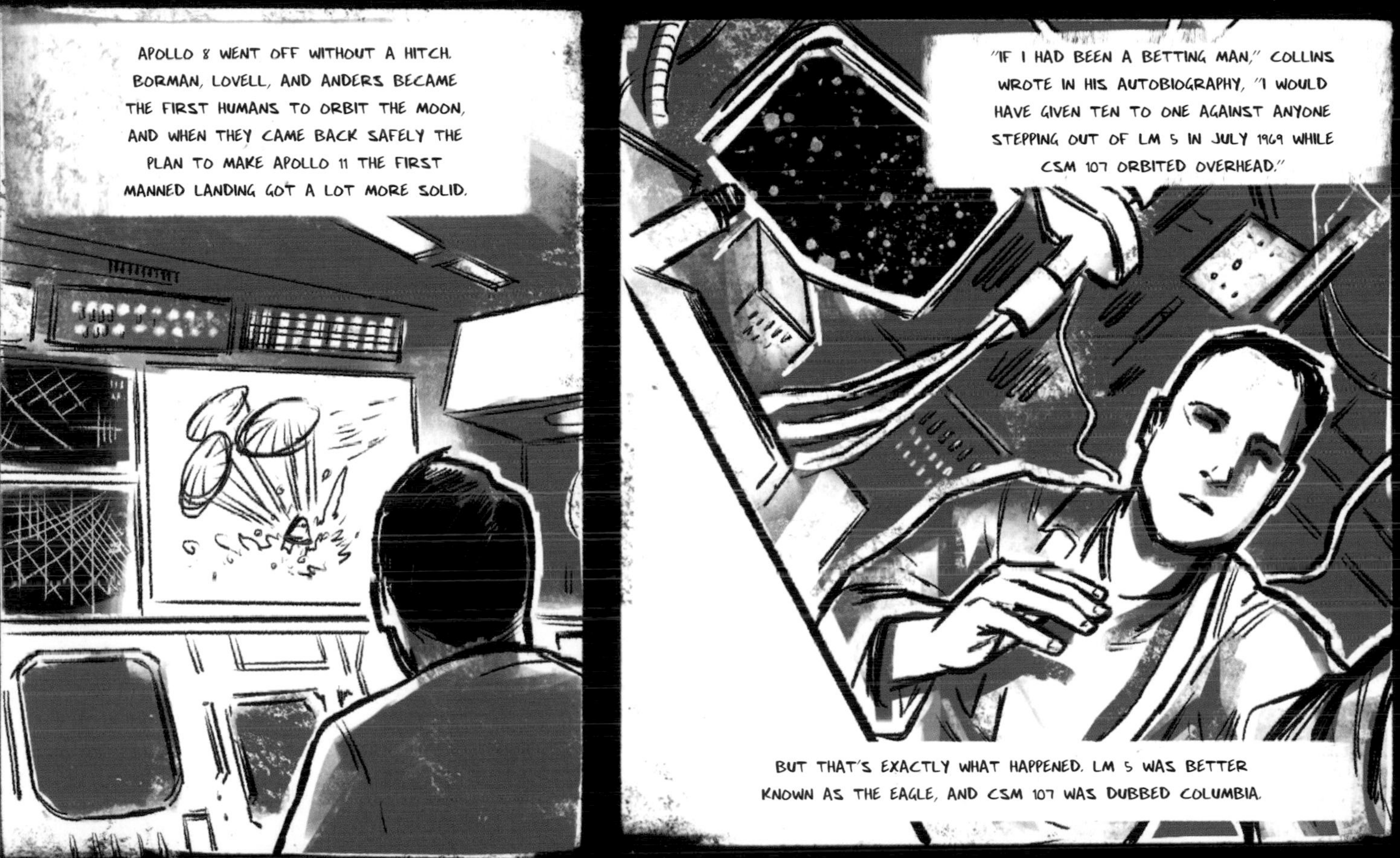
APOLLO 8 WENT OFF WITHOUT A HITCH. BORMAN, LOVELL, AND ANDERS BECAME THE FIRST HUMANS TO ORBIT THE MOON, AND WHEN THEY CAME BACK SAFELY THE PLAN TO MAKE APOLLO 11 THE FIRST MANNED LANDING GOT A LOT MORE SOLID.
"IF I HAD BEEN A BETTING MAN," COLLINS WROTE IN HIS AUTOBIOGRAPHY, "I WOULD HAVE GIVEN TEN TO ONE AGAINST ANYONE STEPPING OUT OF LM 5 IN JULY 1969 WHILE CSM 107 ORBITED OVERHEAD."
BUT THAT'S EXACTLY WHAT HAPPENED. LM 5 WAS BETTER KNOWN AS THE EAGLE, AND CSM 107 WAS DUBBED COLUMBIA.

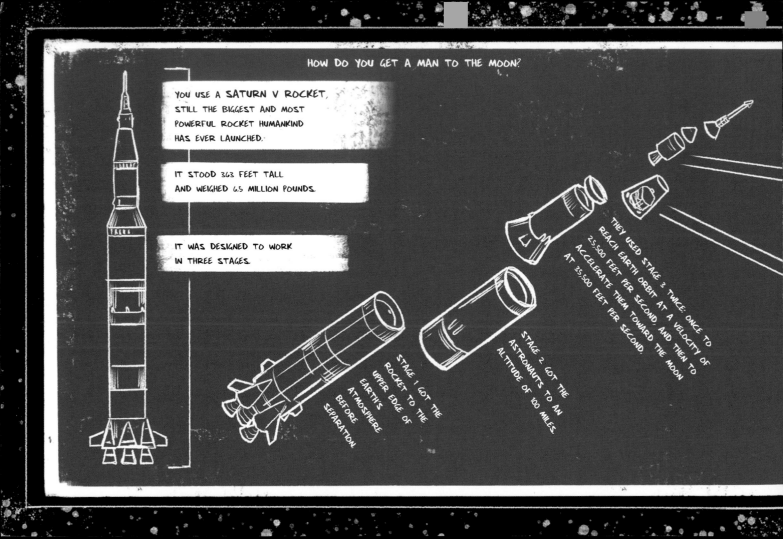

HOW DO YOU GET A MAN TO THE MOON?

YOU USE A **SATURN V ROCKET**, STILL THE BIGGEST AND MOST POWERFUL ROCKET HUMANKIND HAS EVER LAUNCHED.

IT STOOD 363 FEET TALL AND WEIGHED 6.5 MILLION POUNDS.

IT WAS DESIGNED TO WORK IN THREE STAGES.

STAGE 1 GOT THE ROCKET TO THE UPPER EDGE OF EARTH'S ATMOSPHERE BEFORE SEPARATION

STAGE 2 GOT THE ASTRONAUTS TO AN ALTITUDE OF 100 MILES

THEY USED STAGE 3 TWICE: ONCE TO REACH EARTH ORBIT AT A VELOCITY OF 25,500 FEET PER SECOND, AND THEN TO ACCELERATE THEM TOWARD THE MOON AT 35,500 FEET PER SECOND.

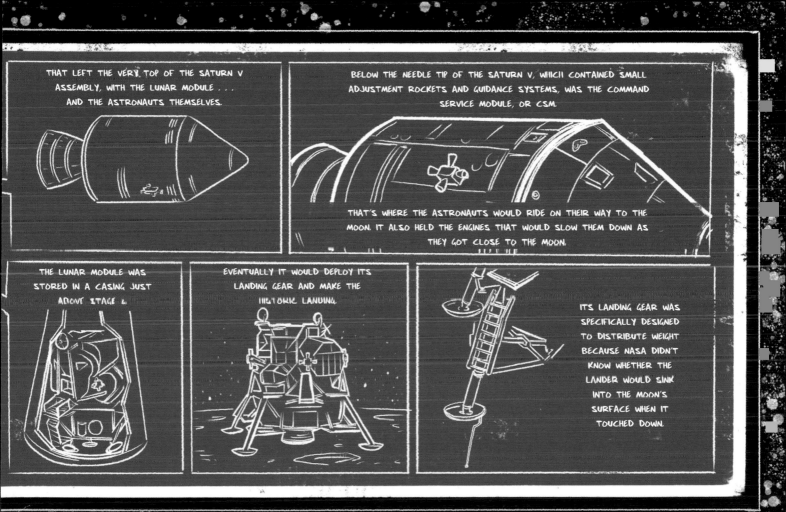

THAT LEFT THE VERY TOP OF THE SATURN V ASSEMBLY, WITH THE LUNAR MODULE . . . AND THE ASTRONAUTS THEMSELVES.

BELOW THE NEEDLE TIP OF THE SATURN V, WHICH CONTAINED SMALL ADJUSTMENT ROCKETS AND GUIDANCE SYSTEMS, WAS THE COMMAND SERVICE MODULE, OR CSM.

THAT'S WHERE THE ASTRONAUTS WOULD RIDE ON THEIR WAY TO THE MOON. IT ALSO HELD THE ENGINES THAT WOULD SLOW THEM DOWN AS THEY GOT CLOSE TO THE MOON.

THE LUNAR MODULE WAS STORED IN A CASING JUST ABOVE STAGE 2.

EVENTUALLY IT WOULD DEPLOY ITS LANDING GEAR AND MAKE THE HISTORIC LANDING.

ITS LANDING GEAR WAS SPECIFICALLY DESIGNED TO DISTRIBUTE WEIGHT BECAUSE NASA DIDN'T KNOW WHETHER THE LANDER WOULD SINK INTO THE MOON'S SURFACE WHEN IT TOUCHED DOWN.

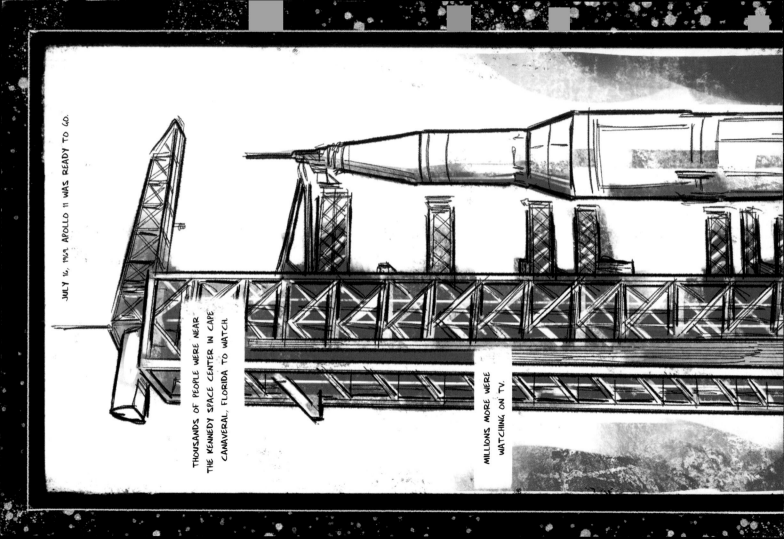

JULY 16, 1969. APOLLO 11 WAS READY TO GO.

THOUSANDS OF PEOPLE WERE NEAR THE KENNEDY SPACE CENTER IN CAPE CANAVERAL, FLORIDA TO WATCH.

MILLIONS MORE WERE WATCHING ON TV.

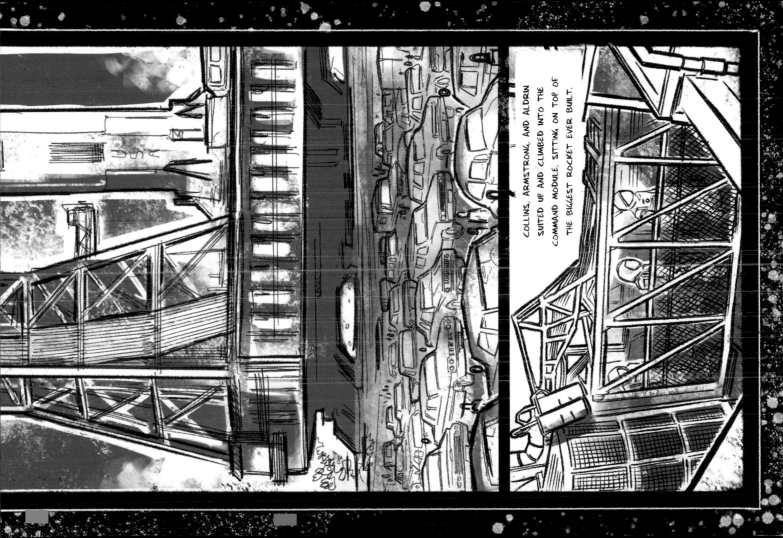

COLLINS, ARMSTRONG, AND ALDRIN SUITED UP AND CLIMBED INTO THE COMMAND MODULE, SITTING ON TOP OF THE BIGGEST ROCKET EVER BUILT.

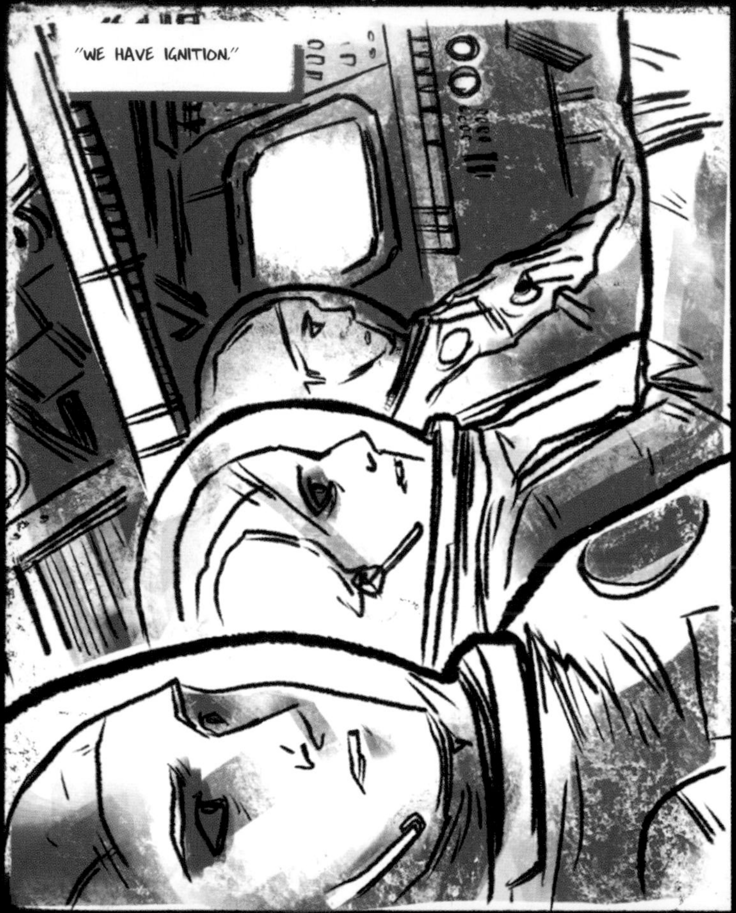
"WE HAVE IGNITION."

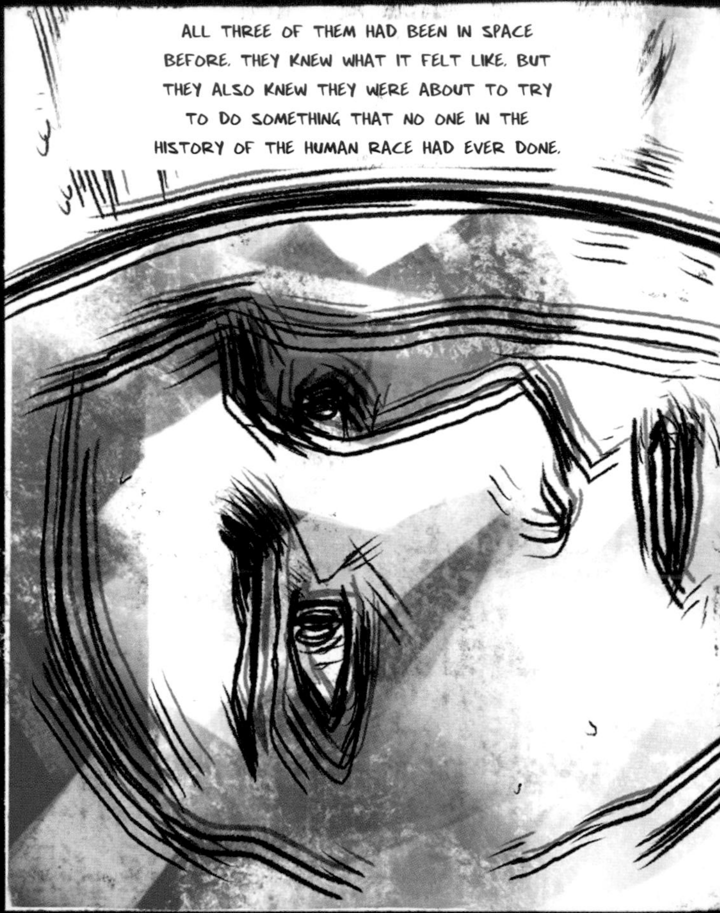
ALL THREE OF THEM HAD BEEN IN SPACE BEFORE. THEY KNEW WHAT IT FELT LIKE. BUT THEY ALSO KNEW THEY WERE ABOUT TO TRY TO DO SOMETHING THAT NO ONE IN THE HISTORY OF THE HUMAN RACE HAD EVER DONE.

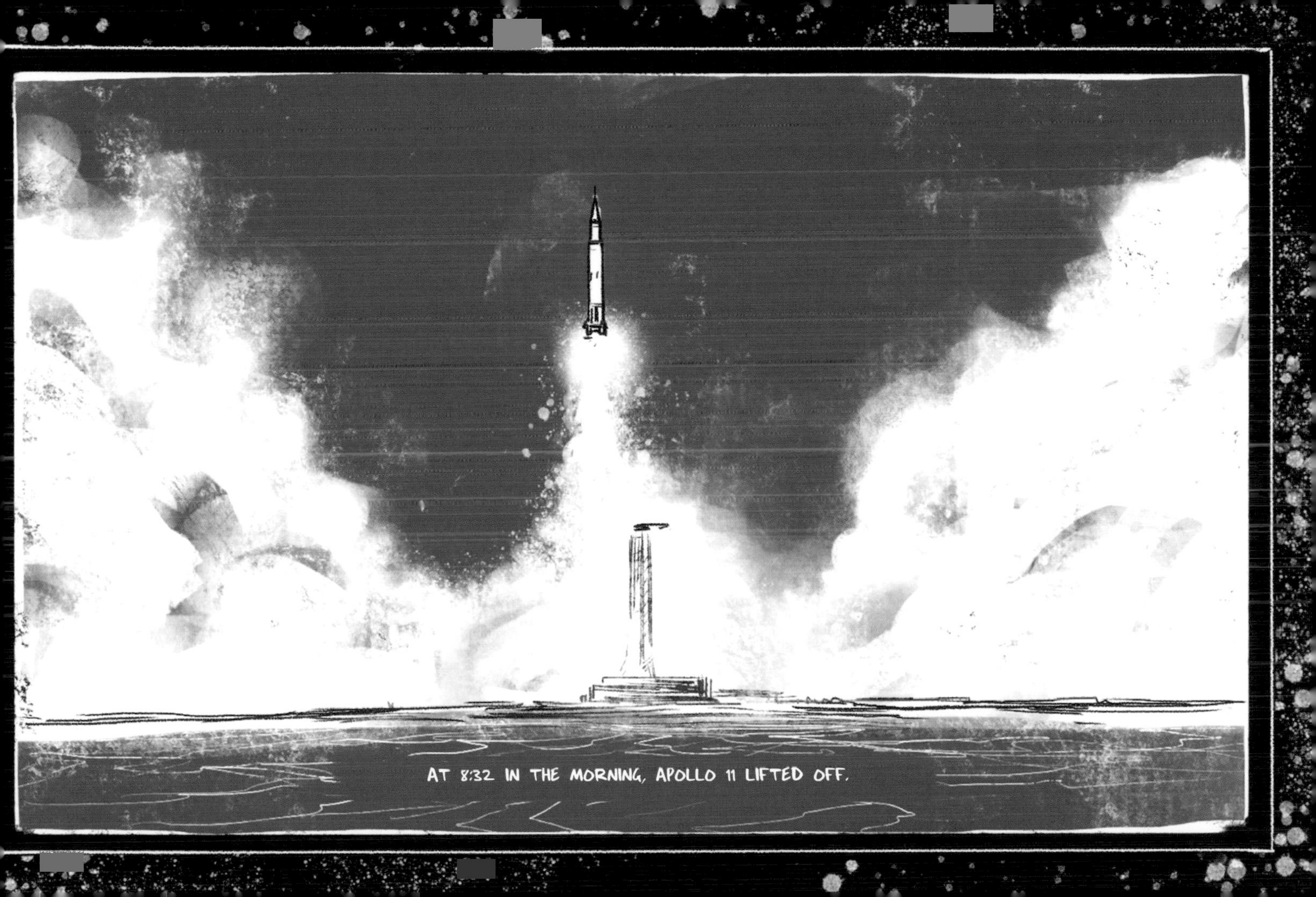
AT 8:32 IN THE MORNING, APOLLO 11 LIFTED OFF.

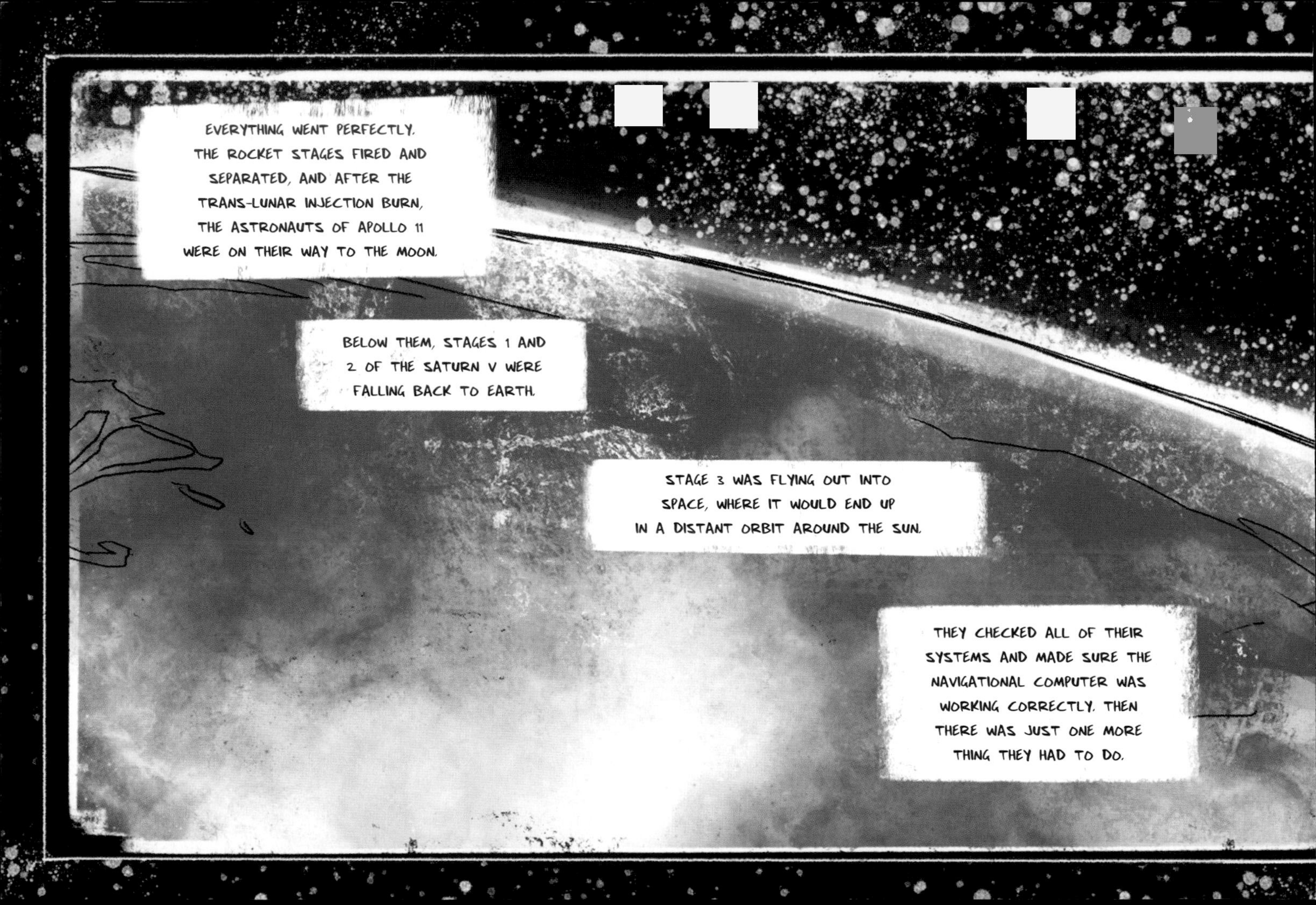
EVERYTHING WENT PERFECTLY. THE ROCKET STAGES FIRED AND SEPARATED, AND AFTER THE TRANS-LUNAR INJECTION BURN, THE ASTRONAUTS OF APOLLO 11 WERE ON THEIR WAY TO THE MOON.
BELOW THEM, STAGES 1 AND 2 OF THE SATURN V WERE FALLING BACK TO EARTH.
STAGE 3 WAS FLYING OUT INTO SPACE, WHERE IT WOULD END UP IN A DISTANT ORBIT AROUND THE SUN.
THEY CHECKED ALL OF THEIR SYSTEMS AND MADE SURE THE NAVIGATIONAL COMPUTER WAS WORKING CORRECTLY. THEN THERE WAS JUST ONE MORE THING THEY HAD TO DO.

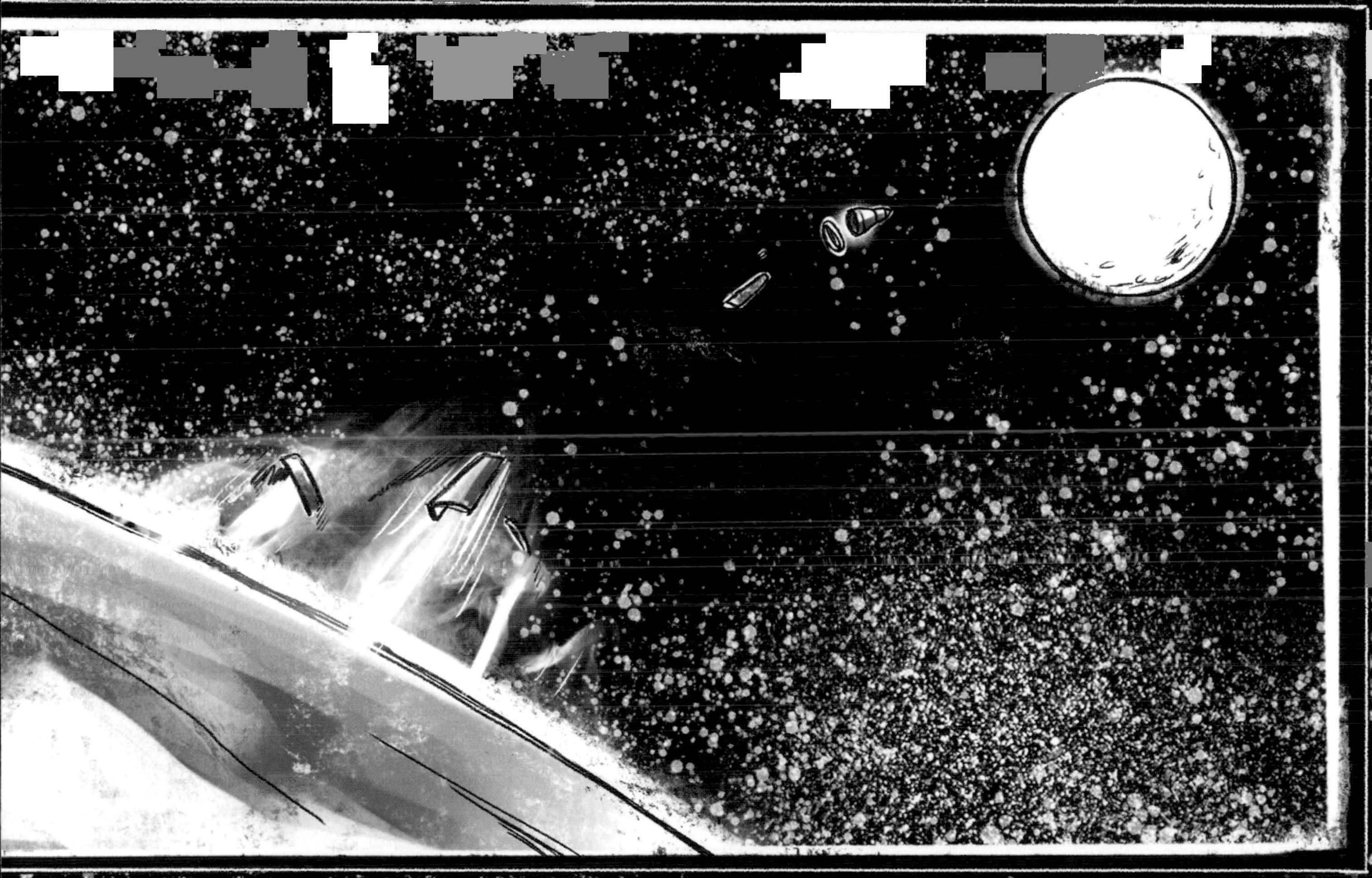

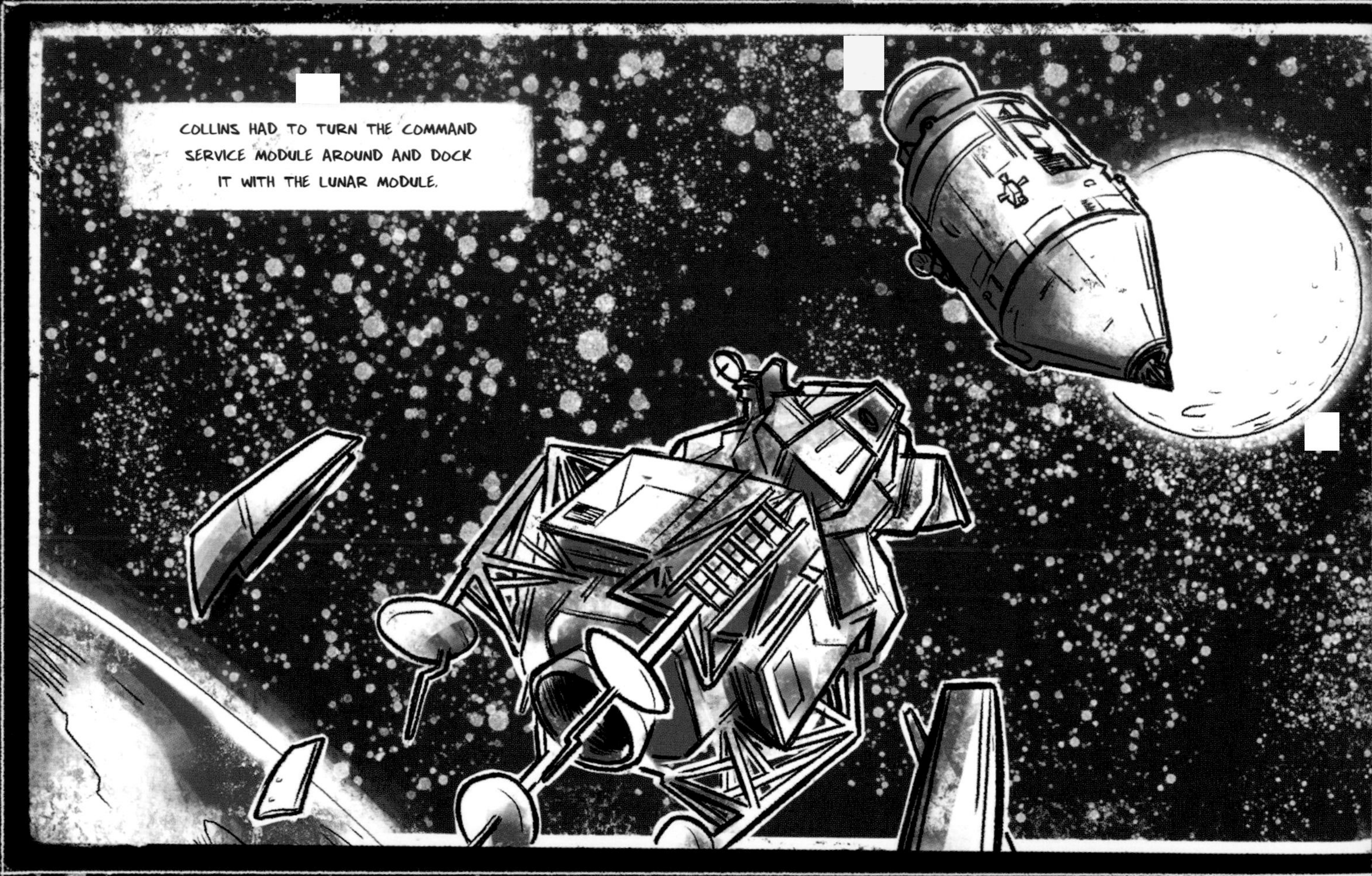
COLLINS HAD TO TURN THE COMMAND SERVICE MODULE AROUND AND DOCK IT WITH THE LUNAR MODULE.

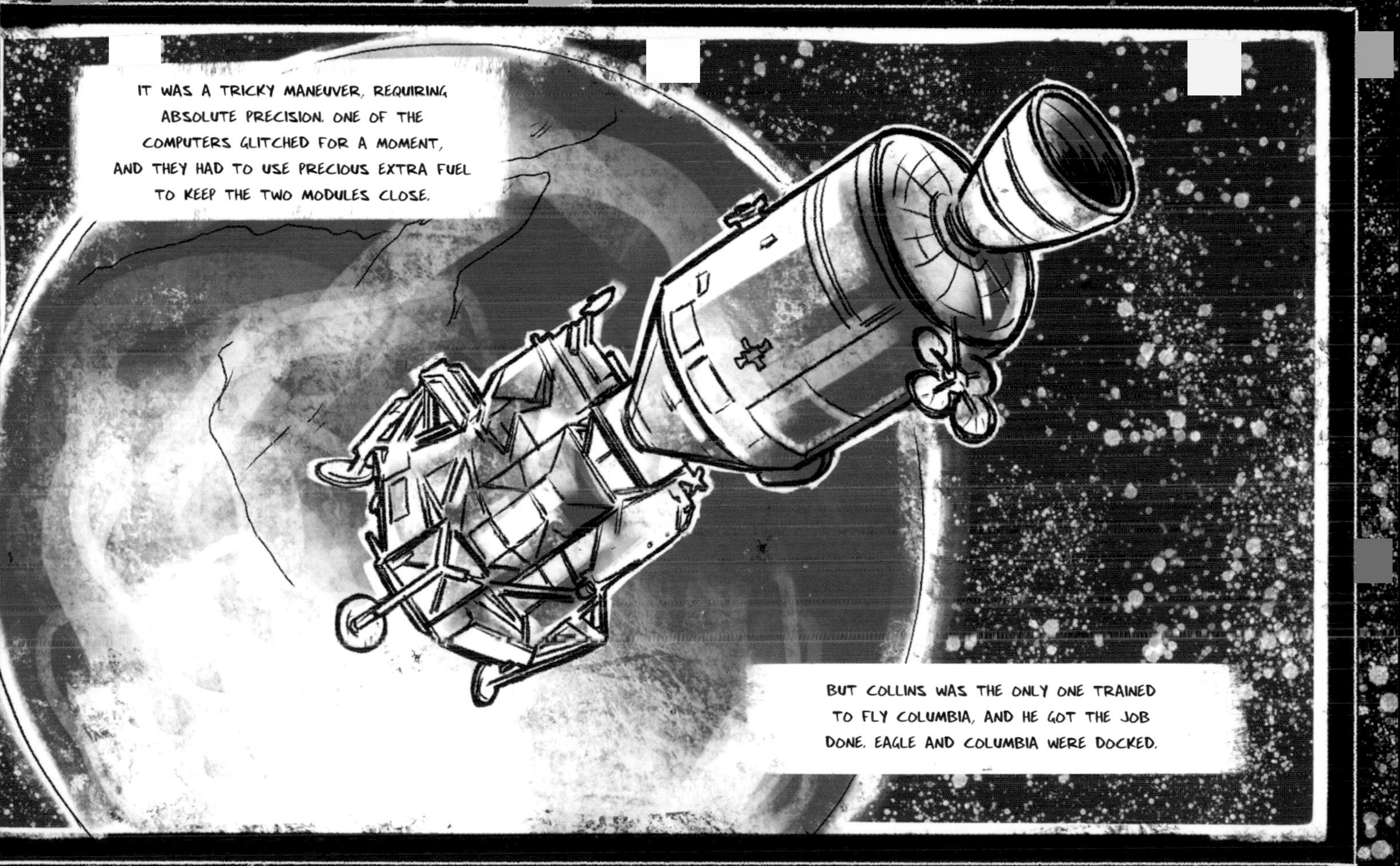
IT WAS A TRICKY MANEUVER, REQUIRING ABSOLUTE PRECISION. ONE OF THE COMPUTERS GLITCHED FOR A MOMENT, AND THEY HAD TO USE PRECIOUS EXTRA FUEL TO KEEP THE TWO MODULES CLOSE.
BUT COLLINS WAS THE ONLY ONE TRAINED TO FLY COLUMBIA, AND HE GOT THE JOB DONE. EAGLE AND COLUMBIA WERE DOCKED.

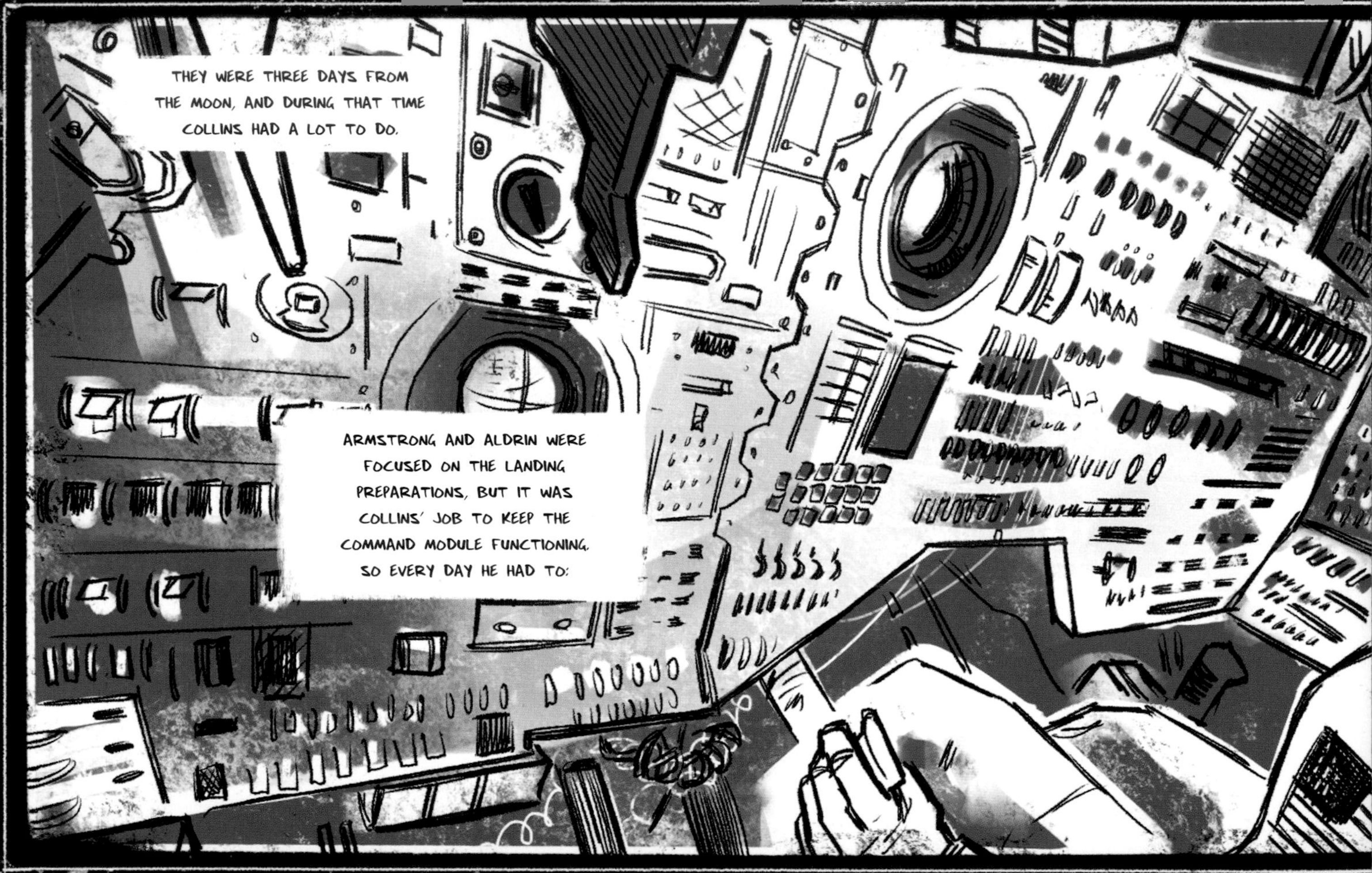
THEY WERE THREE DAYS FROM THE MOON, AND DURING THAT TIME COLLINS HAD A LOT TO DO.
ARMSTRONG AND ALDRIN WERE FOCUSED ON THE LANDING PREPARATIONS, BUT IT WAS COLLINS' JOB TO KEEP THE COMMAND MODULE FUNCTIONING, SO EVERY DAY HE HAD TO:

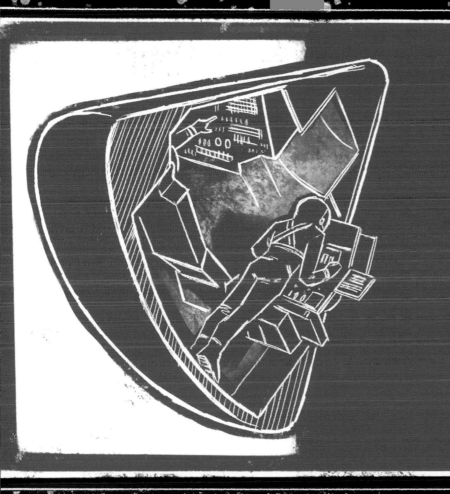

- PURGE FUEL CELLS

- CHARGE BATTERIES

- DUMP WASTE WATER

- CHARGE CO2 CANISTERS

- PREPARE FOOD

- CHLORINATE DRINKING WATER

- MAKE MID-COURSE CORRECTIONS

- EXERCISE

- TAKE PHOTOGRAPHS

- GET TV CAMERA FOOTAGE OF EARTH AND SPACE

- OH, AND GET SOME SLEEP!

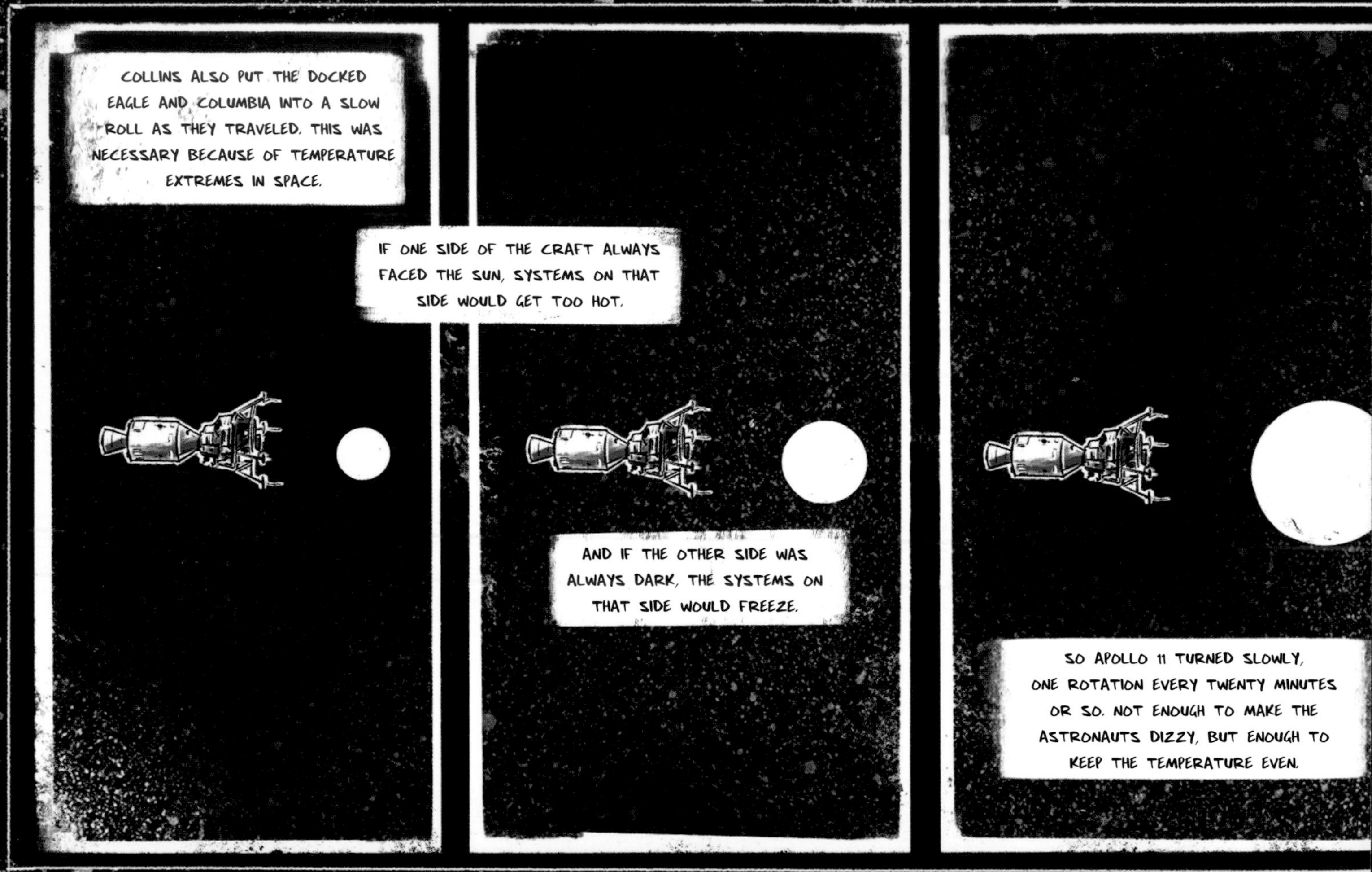
COLLINS ALSO PUT THE DOCKED EAGLE AND COLUMBIA INTO A SLOW ROLL AS THEY TRAVELED. THIS WAS NECESSARY BECAUSE OF TEMPERATURE EXTREMES IN SPACE.
IF ONE SIDE OF THE CRAFT ALWAYS FACED THE SUN, SYSTEMS ON THAT SIDE WOULD GET TOO HOT.
AND IF THE OTHER SIDE WAS ALWAYS DARK, THE SYSTEMS ON THAT SIDE WOULD FREEZE.
SO APOLLO 11 TURNED SLOWLY, ONE ROTATION EVERY TWENTY MINUTES OR SO. NOT ENOUGH TO MAKE THE ASTRONAUTS DIZZY, BUT ENOUGH TO KEEP THE TEMPERATURE EVEN.

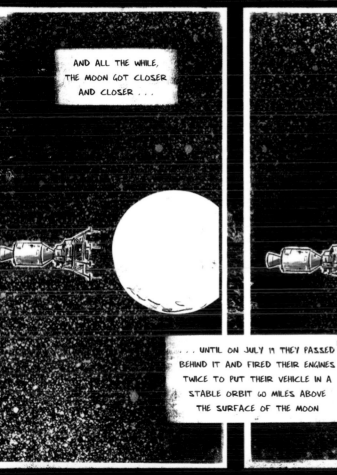

AND ALL THE WHILE, THE MOON GOT CLOSER AND CLOSER . . .

. . . UNTIL ON JULY 19 THEY PASSED BEHIND IT AND FIRED THEIR ENGINES TWICE TO PUT THEIR VEHICLE IN A STABLE ORBIT 60 MILES ABOVE THE SURFACE OF THE MOON

TOMORROW THEY WOULD TRY TO BECOME THE FIRST HUMANS IN HISTORY TO LAND ON THE SURFACE OF ANOTHER WORLD.

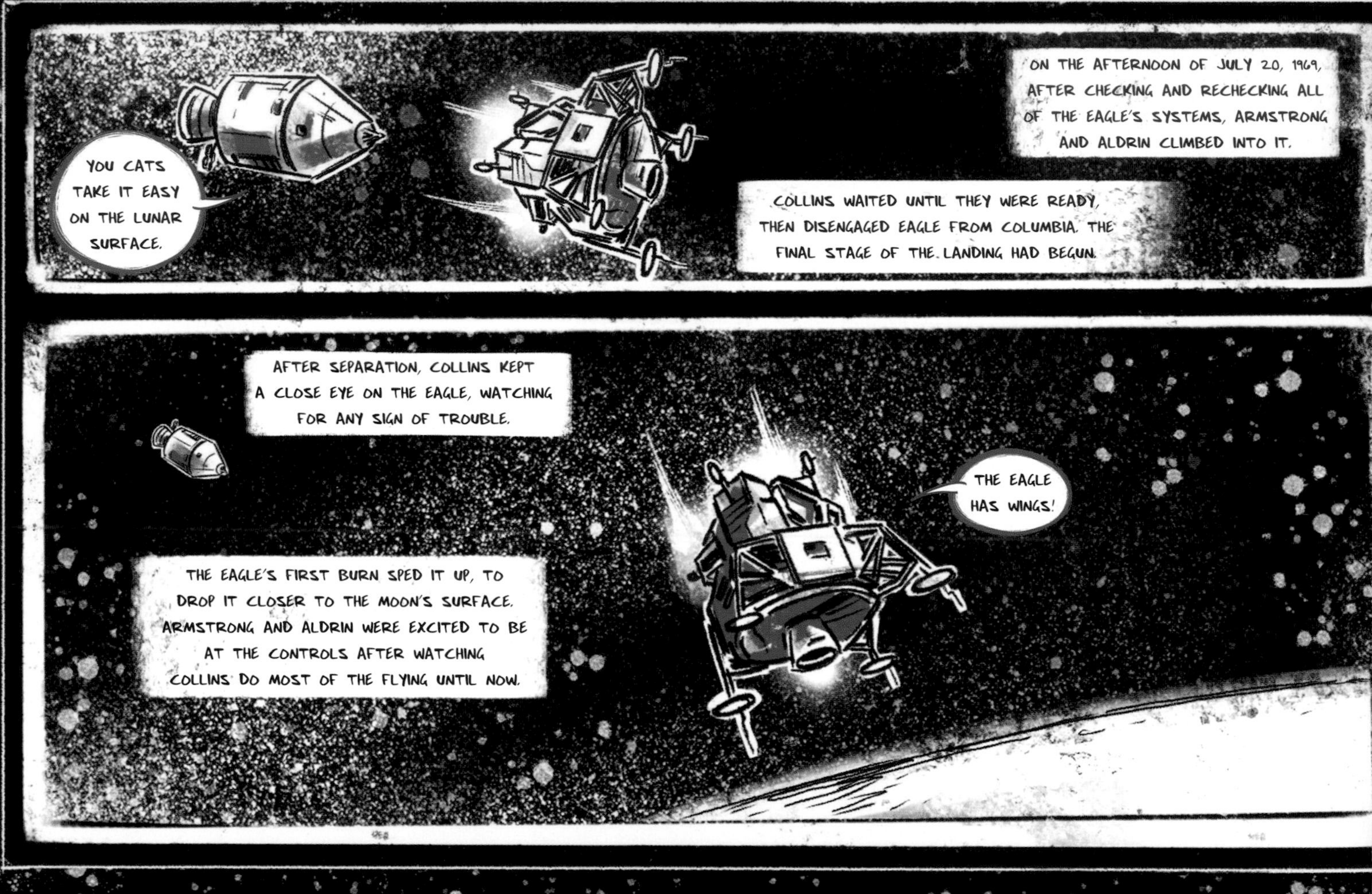
ON THE AFTERNOON OF JULY 20, 1969, AFTER CHECKING AND RECHECKING ALL OF THE EAGLE'S SYSTEMS, ARMSTRONG AND ALDRIN CLIMBED INTO IT.
YOU CATS TAKE IT EASY ON THE LUNAR SURFACE.
COLLINS WAITED UNTIL THEY WERE READY, THEN DISENGAGED EAGLE FROM COLUMBIA. THE FINAL STAGE OF THE LANDING HAD BEGUN.
AFTER SEPARATION, COLLINS KEPT A CLOSE EYE ON THE EAGLE, WATCHING FOR ANY SIGN OF TROUBLE.
THE EAGLE HAS WINGS!
THE EAGLE'S FIRST BURN SPED IT UP, TO DROP IT CLOSER TO THE MOON'S SURFACE. ARMSTRONG AND ALDRIN WERE EXCITED TO BE AT THE CONTROLS AFTER WATCHING COLLINS DO MOST OF THE FLYING UNTIL NOW.

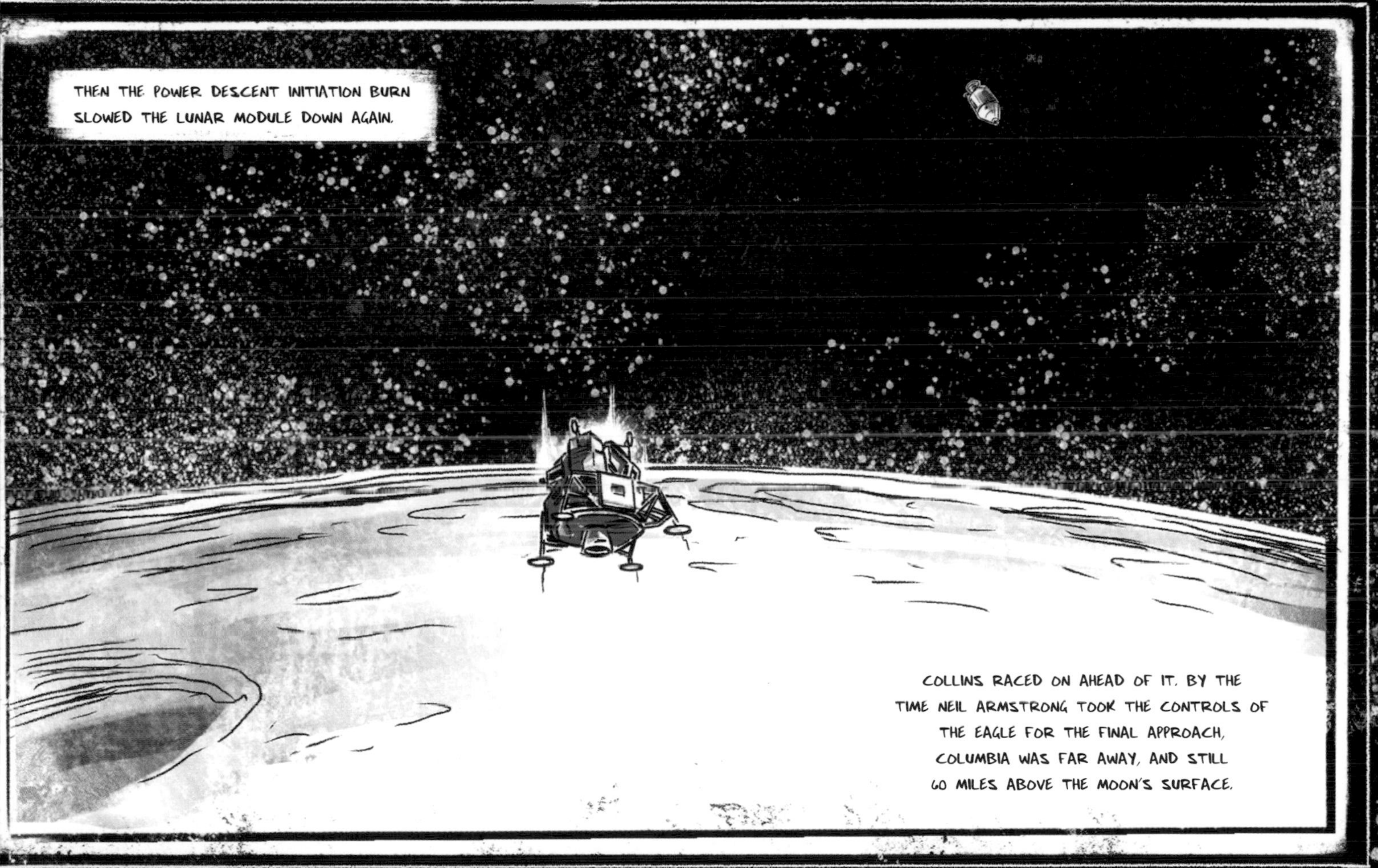

THEN THE POWER DESCENT INITIATION BURN SLOWED THE LUNAR MODULE DOWN AGAIN.
COLLINS RACED ON AHEAD OF IT. BY THE TIME NEIL ARMSTRONG TOOK THE CONTROLS OF THE EAGLE FOR THE FINAL APPROACH, COLUMBIA WAS FAR AWAY, AND STILL 60 MILES ABOVE THE MOON'S SURFACE.

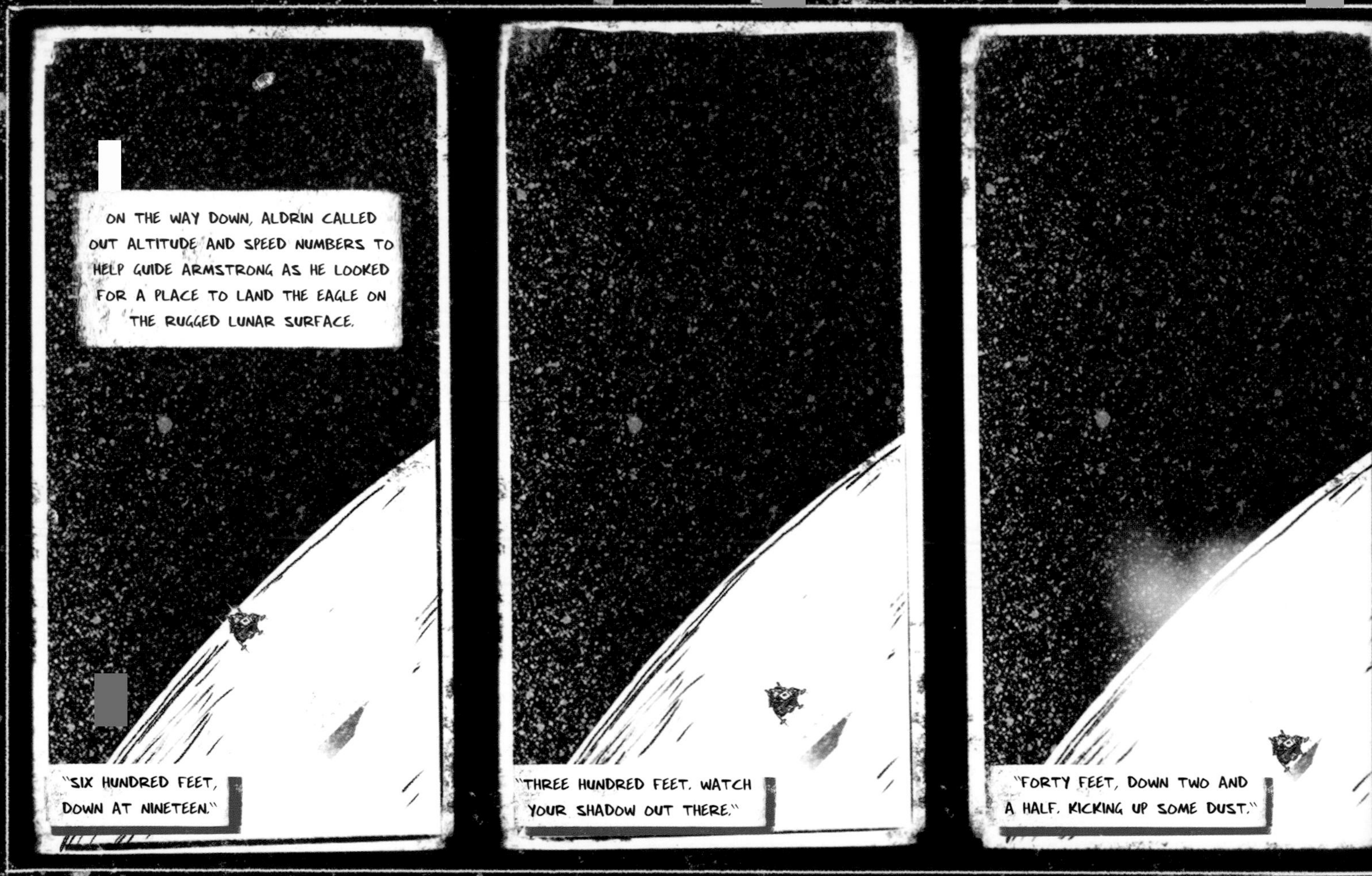
ON THE WAY DOWN, ALDRIN CALLED OUT ALTITUDE AND SPEED NUMBERS TO HELP GUIDE ARMSTRONG AS HE LOOKED FOR A PLACE TO LAND THE EAGLE ON THE RUGGED LUNAR SURFACE.
"SIX HUNDRED FEET, DOWN AT NINETEEN."
"THREE HUNDRED FEET. WATCH YOUR SHADOW OUT THERE."
"FORTY FEET, DOWN TWO AND A HALF. KICKING UP SOME DUST."

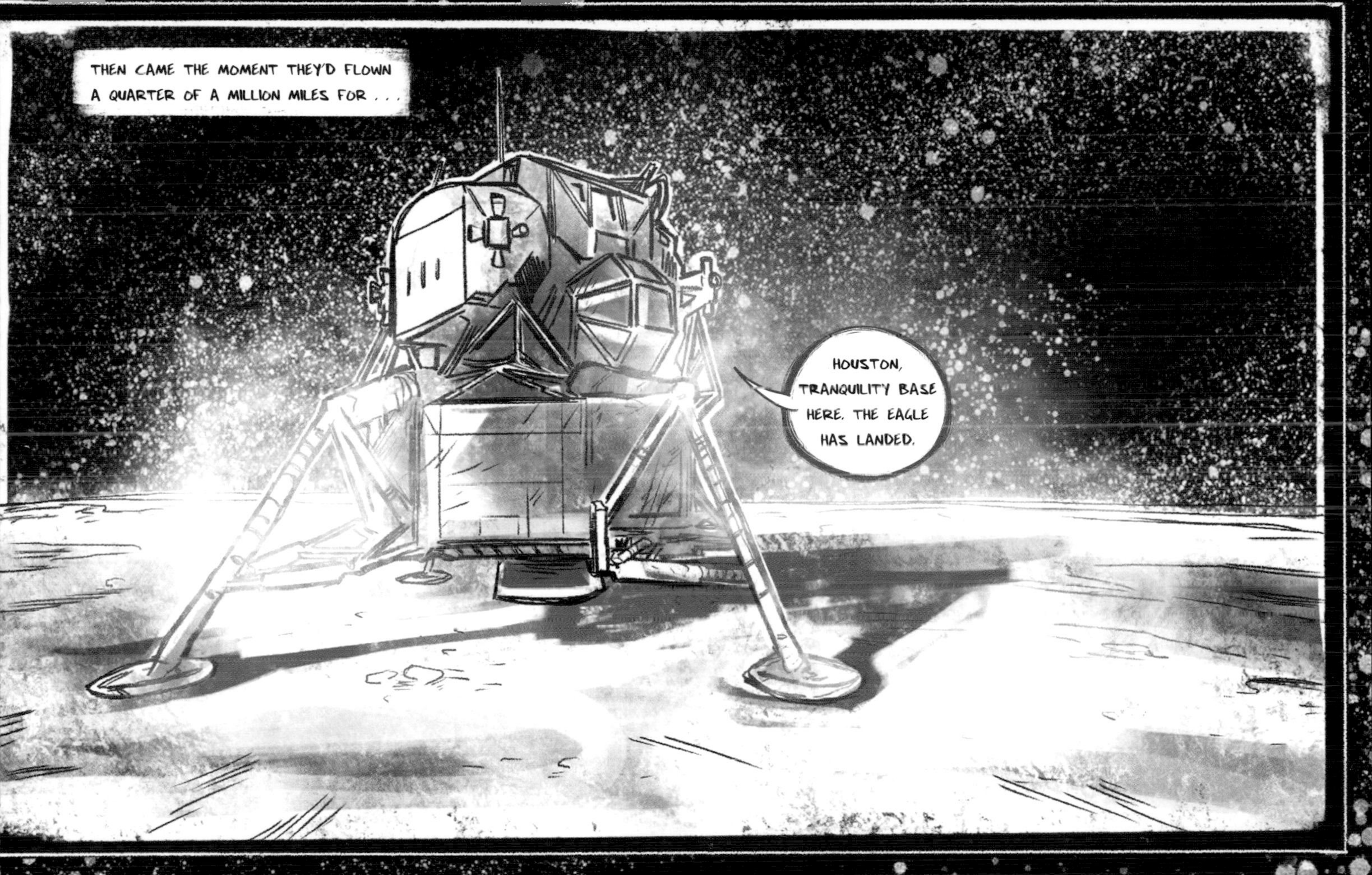
THEN CAME THE MOMENT THEY'D FLOWN A QUARTER OF A MILLION MILES FOR . . .
HOUSTON, TRANQUILITY BASE HERE. THE EAGLE HAS LANDED.

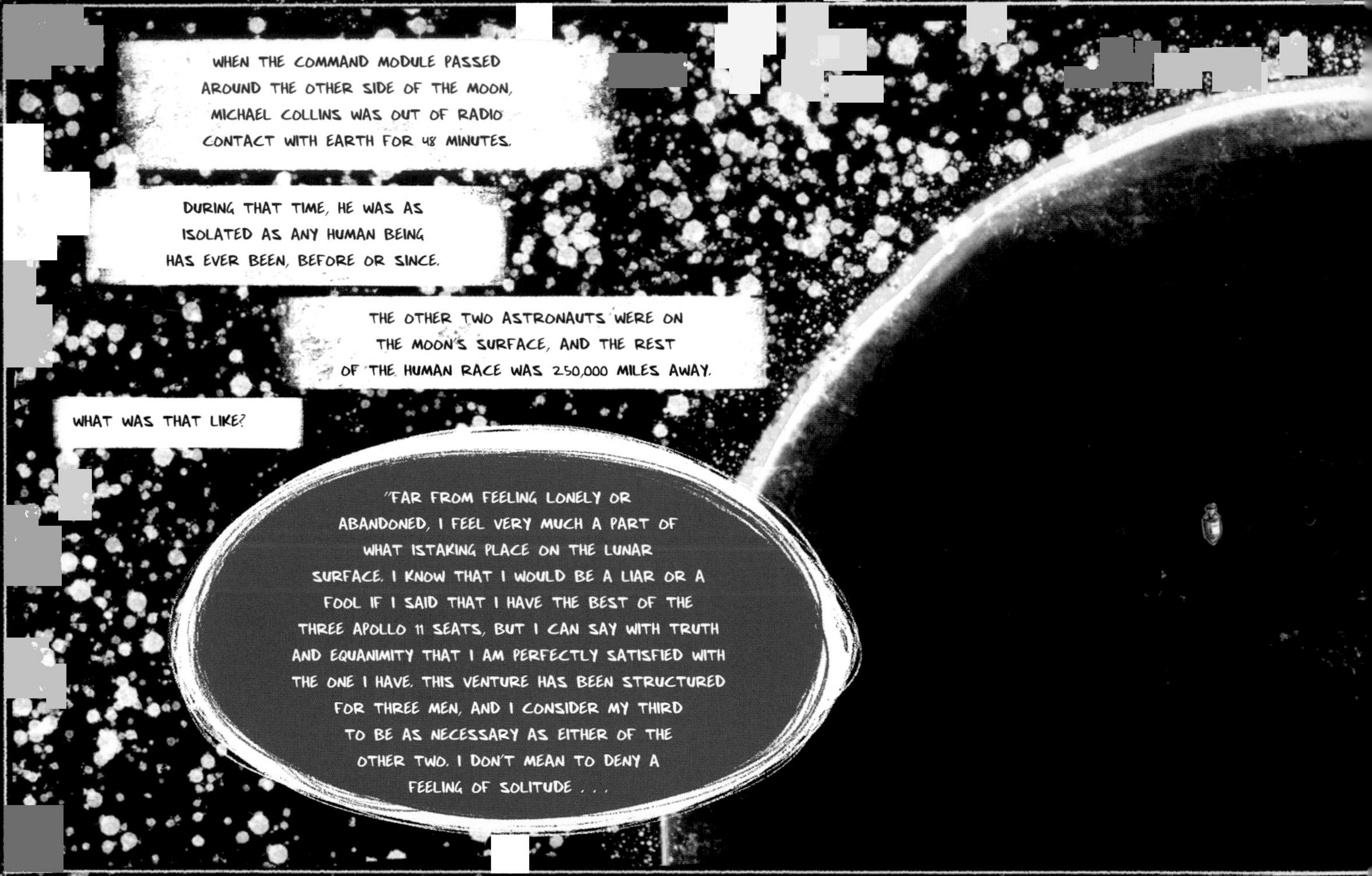
WHEN THE COMMAND MODULE PASSED AROUND THE OTHER SIDE OF THE MOON, MICHAEL COLLINS WAS OUT OF RADIO CONTACT WITH EARTH FOR 48 MINUTES.
DURING THAT TIME, HE WAS AS ISOLATED AS ANY HUMAN BEING HAS EVER BEEN, BEFORE OR SINCE.
THE OTHER TWO ASTRONAUTS WERE ON THE MOON'S SURFACE, AND THE REST OF THE HUMAN RACE WAS 250,000 MILES AWAY.
WHAT WAS THAT LIKE?
"FAR FROM FEELING LONELY OR ABANDONED, I FEEL VERY MUCH A PART OF WHAT ISTAKING PLACE ON THE LUNAR SURFACE. I KNOW THAT I WOULD BE A LIAR OR A FOOL IF I SAID THAT I HAVE THE BEST OF THE THREE APOLLO 11 SEATS, BUT I CAN SAY WITH TRUTH AND EQUANIMITY THAT I AM PERFECTLY SATISFIED WITH THE ONE I HAVE. THIS VENTURE HAS BEEN STRUCTURED FOR THREE MEN, AND I CONSIDER MY THIRD TO BE AS NECESSARY AS EITHER OF THE OTHER TWO. I DON'T MEAN TO DENY A FEELING OF SOLITUDE . . .

"IT IS THERE,
REINFORCED BY THE FACT
THAT RADIO CONTACT WITH THE
EARTH ABRUPTLY CUTS OFF AT THE
INSTANT I DISAPPEAR BEHIND THE MOON,
I AM ALONE NOW, TRULY ALONE, AND ABSOLUTELY
ISOLATED FROM ANY KNOWN LIFE. I AM IT. IF
A COUNT WERE TAKEN, THE SCORE WOULD BE
THREE BILLION PLUS TWO OVER ON THE
OTHER SIDE OF THE MOON, AND ONE
PLUS GOD KNOWS WHAT
ON THIS SIDE."

HE WOULD MAKE FOURTEEN
ORBITS OF THE MOON WHILE ARMSTRONG
AND ALDRIN WERE ON THE SURFACE.

MOST OF THAT TIME HE SPENT
PREPARING FOR THE RENDEZVOUS
WITH THE LUNAR MODULE.

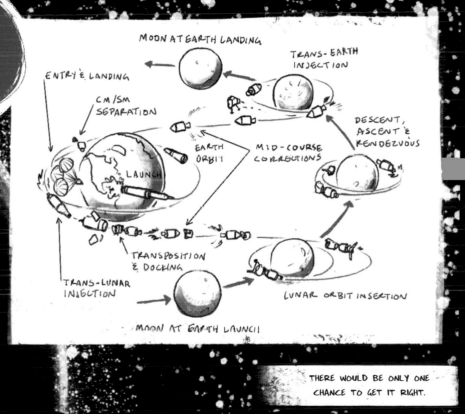

MOON AT EARTH LANDING

TRANS-EARTH
INJECTION

ENTRY & LANDING

CM/SM
SEPARATION

DESCENT,
ASCENT &
RENDEZVOUS

EARTH
ORBIT

MID-COURSE
CORRECTIONS

LAUNCH

TRANSPOSITION
& DOCKING

LUNAR ORBIT INSERTION

TRANS-LUNAR
INJECTION

MOON AT EARTH LAUNCH

THERE WOULD BE ONLY ONE
CHANCE TO GET IT RIGHT.

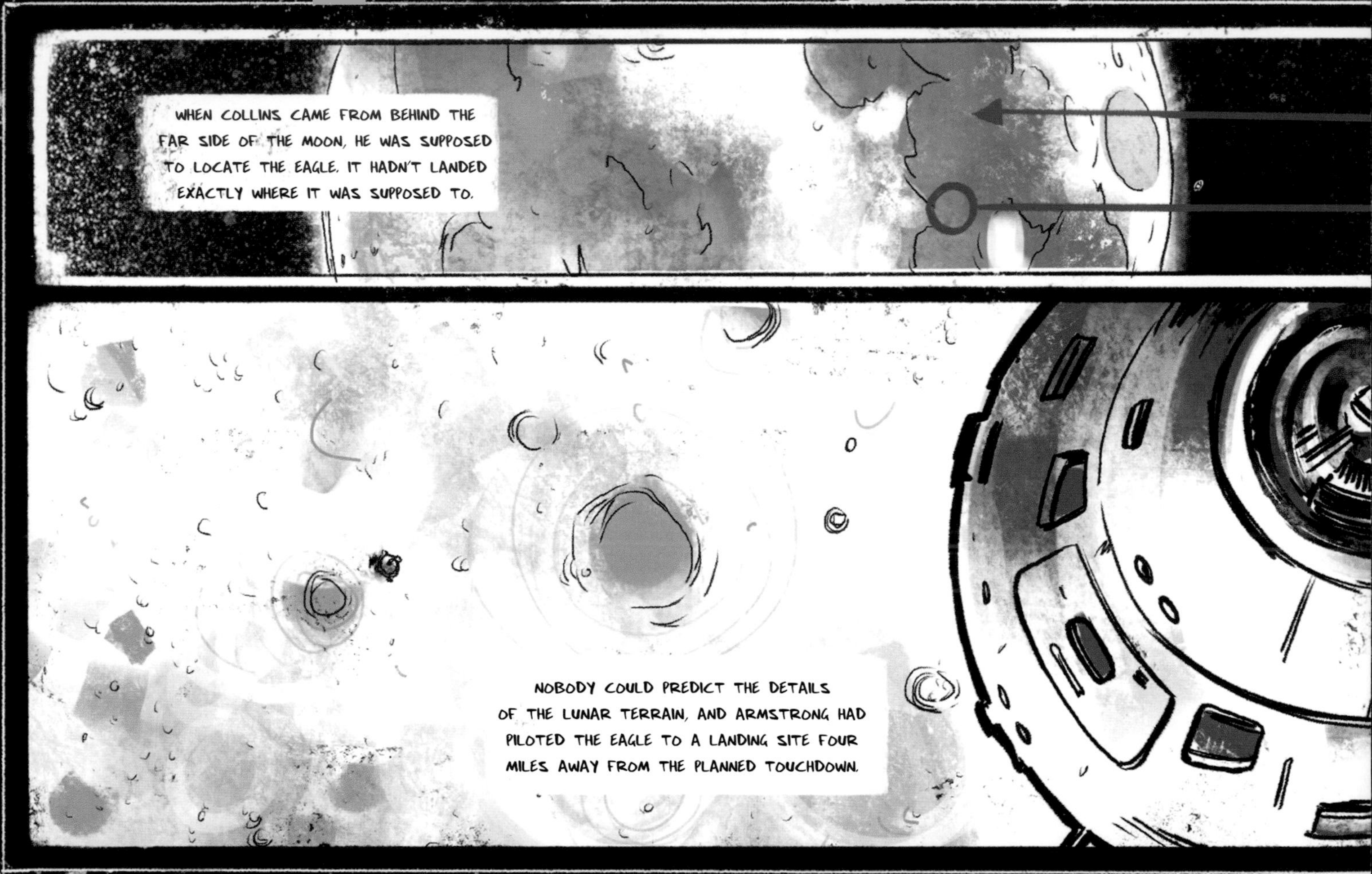
WHEN COLLINS CAME FROM BEHIND THE FAR SIDE OF THE MOON, HE WAS SUPPOSED TO LOCATE THE EAGLE. IT HADN'T LANDED EXACTLY WHERE IT WAS SUPPOSED TO.
NOBODY COULD PREDICT THE DETAILS OF THE LUNAR TERRAIN, AND ARMSTRONG HAD PILOTED THE EAGLE TO A LANDING SITE FOUR MILES AWAY FROM THE PLANNED TOUCHDOWN.

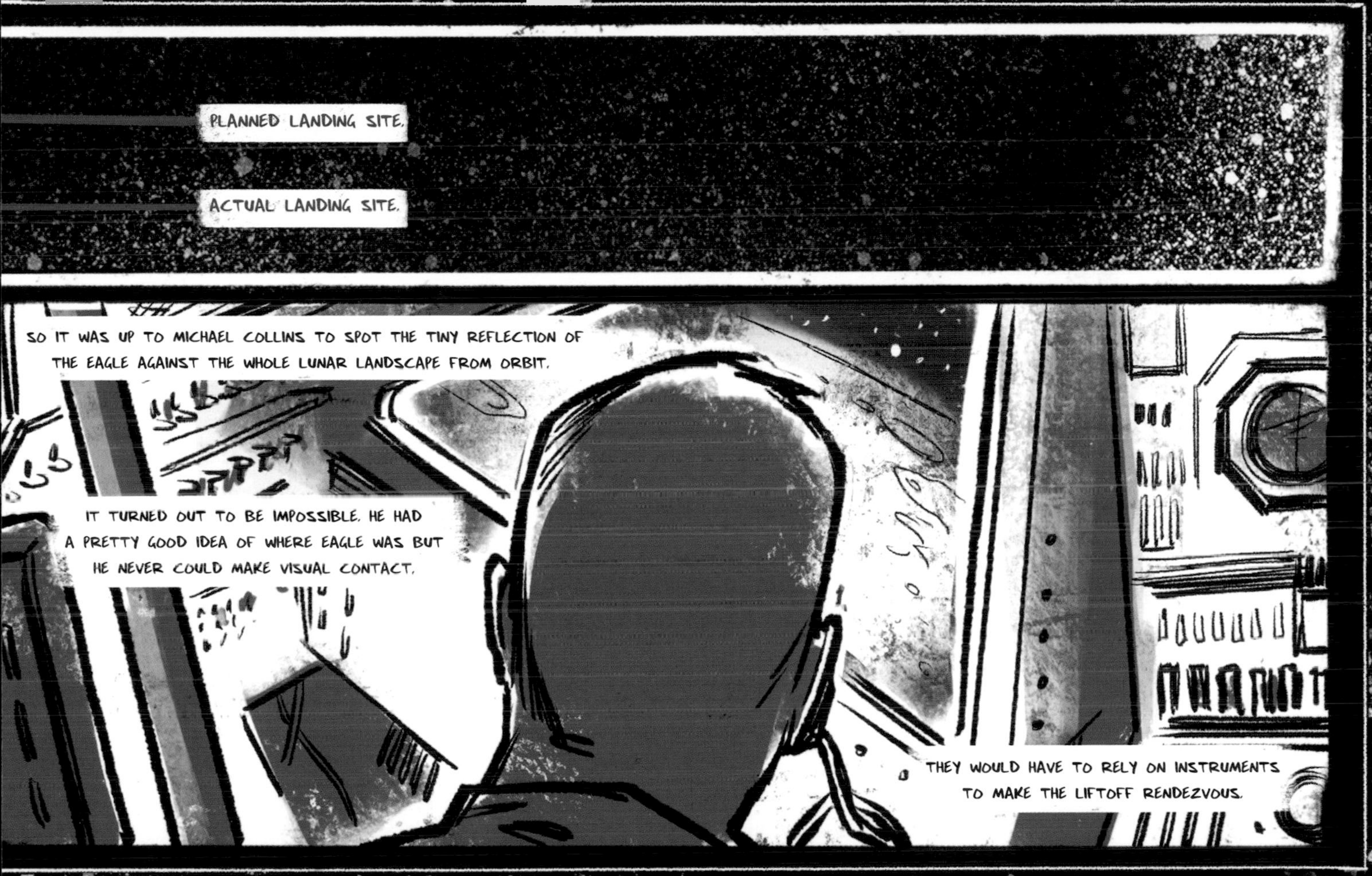
PLANNED LANDING SITE.
ACTUAL LANDING SITE.
SO IT WAS UP TO MICHAEL COLLINS TO SPOT THE TINY REFLECTION OF THE EAGLE AGAINST THE WHOLE LUNAR LANDSCAPE FROM ORBIT.
IT TURNED OUT TO BE IMPOSSIBLE. HE HAD A PRETTY GOOD IDEA OF WHERE EAGLE WAS BUT HE NEVER COULD MAKE VISUAL CONTACT.
THEY WOULD HAVE TO RELY ON INSTRUMENTS TO MAKE THE LIFTOFF RENDEZVOUS.

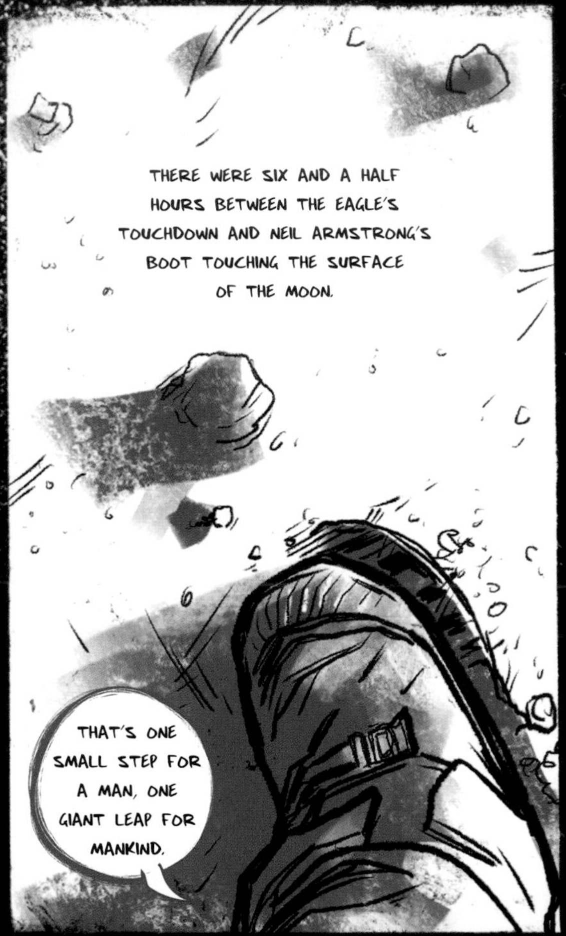
THERE WERE SIX AND A HALF HOURS BETWEEN THE EAGLE'S TOUCHDOWN AND NEIL ARMSTRONG'S BOOT TOUCHING THE SURFACE OF THE MOON.
THAT'S ONE SMALL STEP FOR A MAN, ONE GIANT LEAP FOR MANKIND.

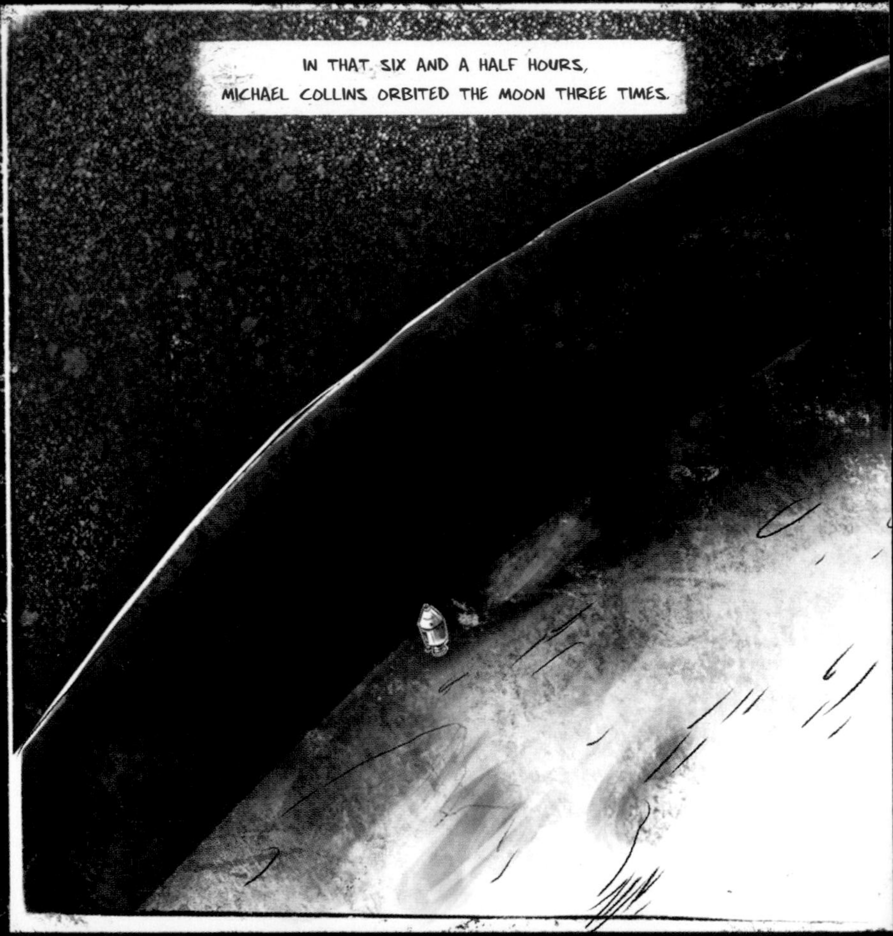
IN THAT SIX AND A HALF HOURS, MICHAEL COLLINS ORBITED THE MOON THREE TIMES.

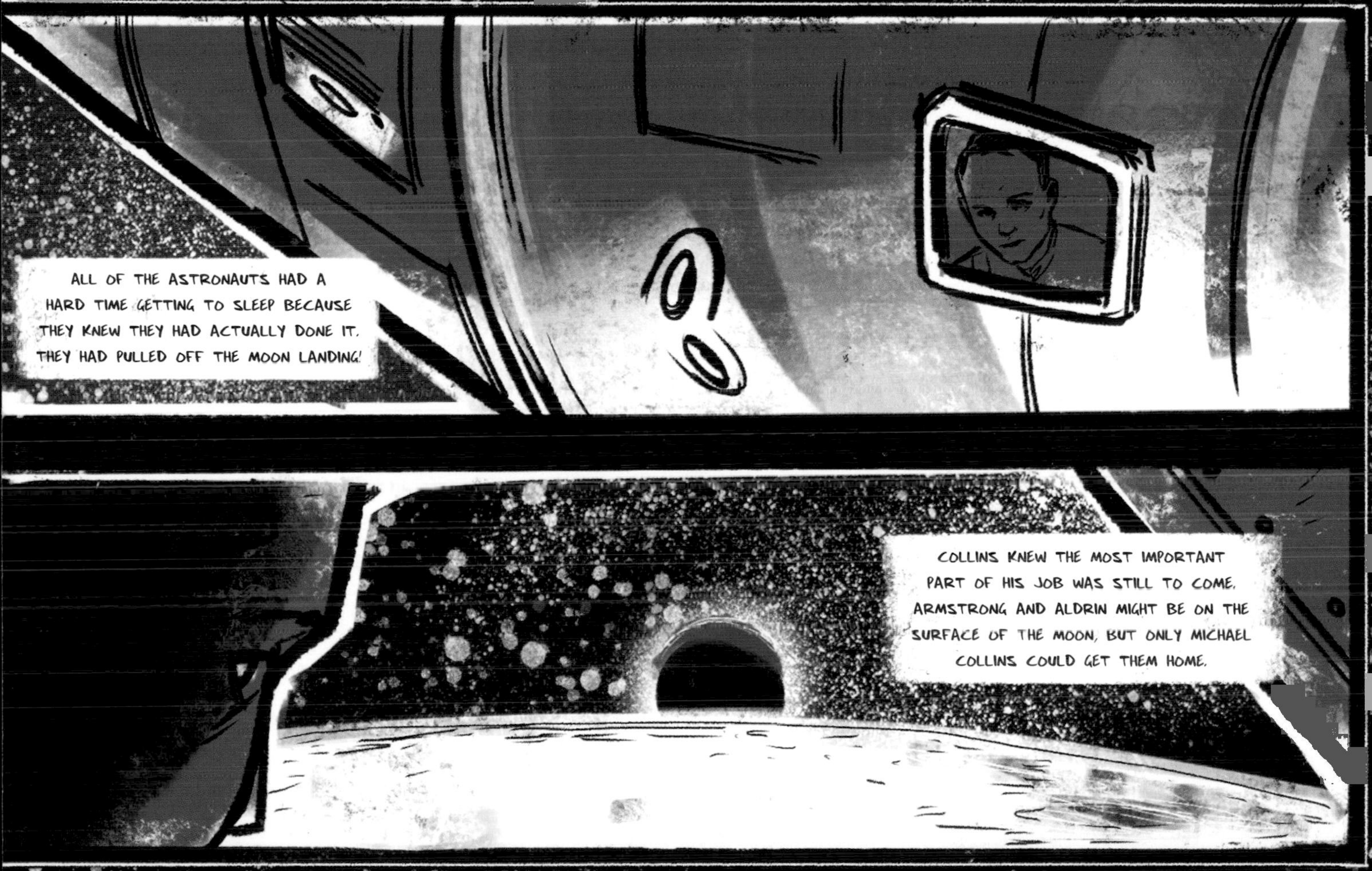
ALL OF THE ASTRONAUTS HAD A HARD TIME GETTING TO SLEEP BECAUSE THEY KNEW THEY HAD ACTUALLY DONE IT. THEY HAD PULLED OFF THE MOON LANDING!
COLLINS KNEW THE MOST IMPORTANT PART OF HIS JOB WAS STILL TO COME. ARMSTRONG AND ALDRIN MIGHT BE ON THE SURFACE OF THE MOON, BUT ONLY MICHAEL COLLINS COULD GET THEM HOME.

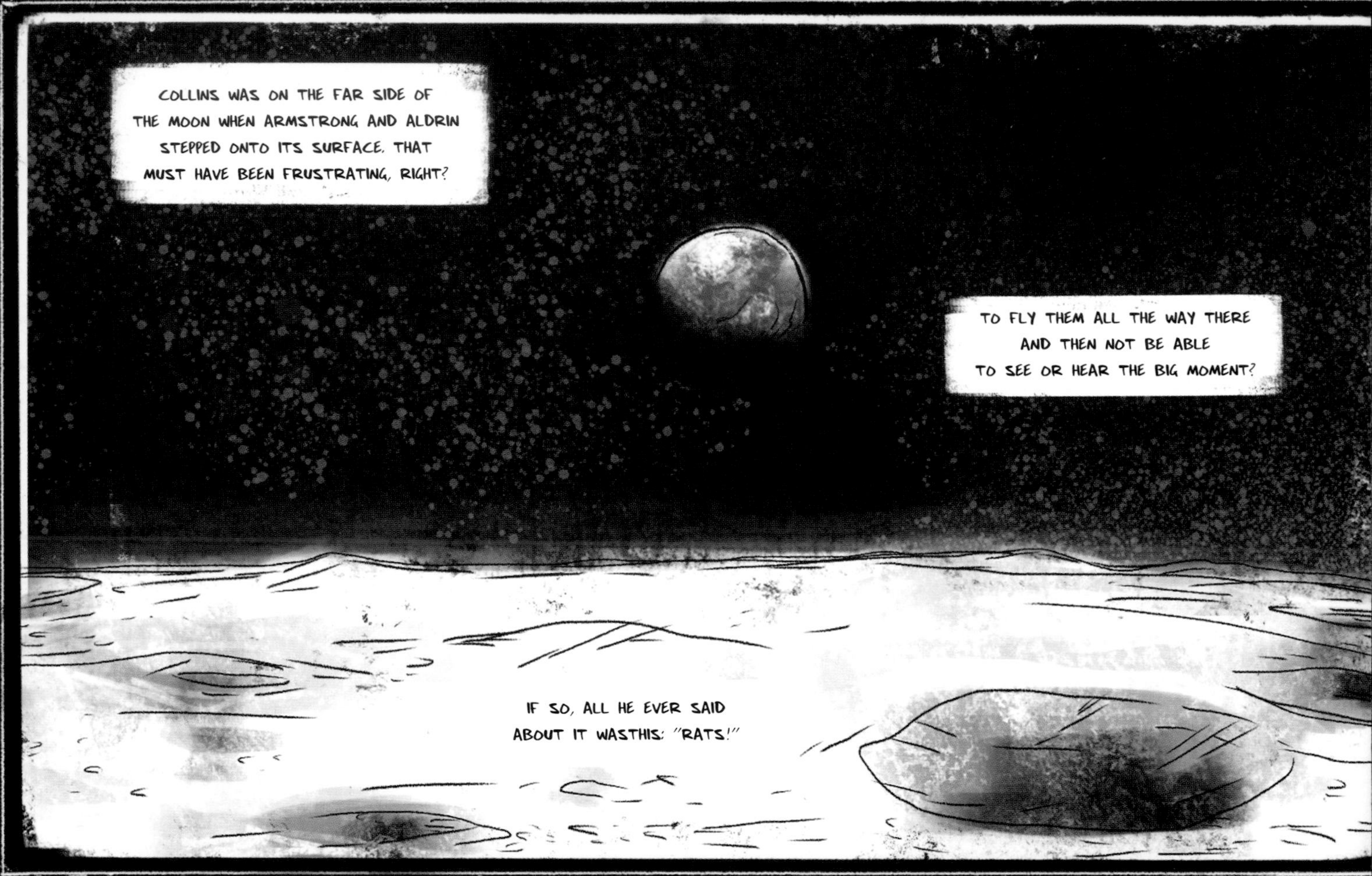
COLLINS WAS ON THE FAR SIDE OF THE MOON WHEN ARMSTRONG AND ALDRIN STEPPED ONTO ITS SURFACE. THAT MUST HAVE BEEN FRUSTRATING, RIGHT?
TO FLY THEM ALL THE WAY THERE AND THEN NOT BE ABLE TO SEE OR HEAR THE BIG MOMENT?
IF SO, ALL HE EVER SAID ABOUT IT WASTHIS: "RATS!"

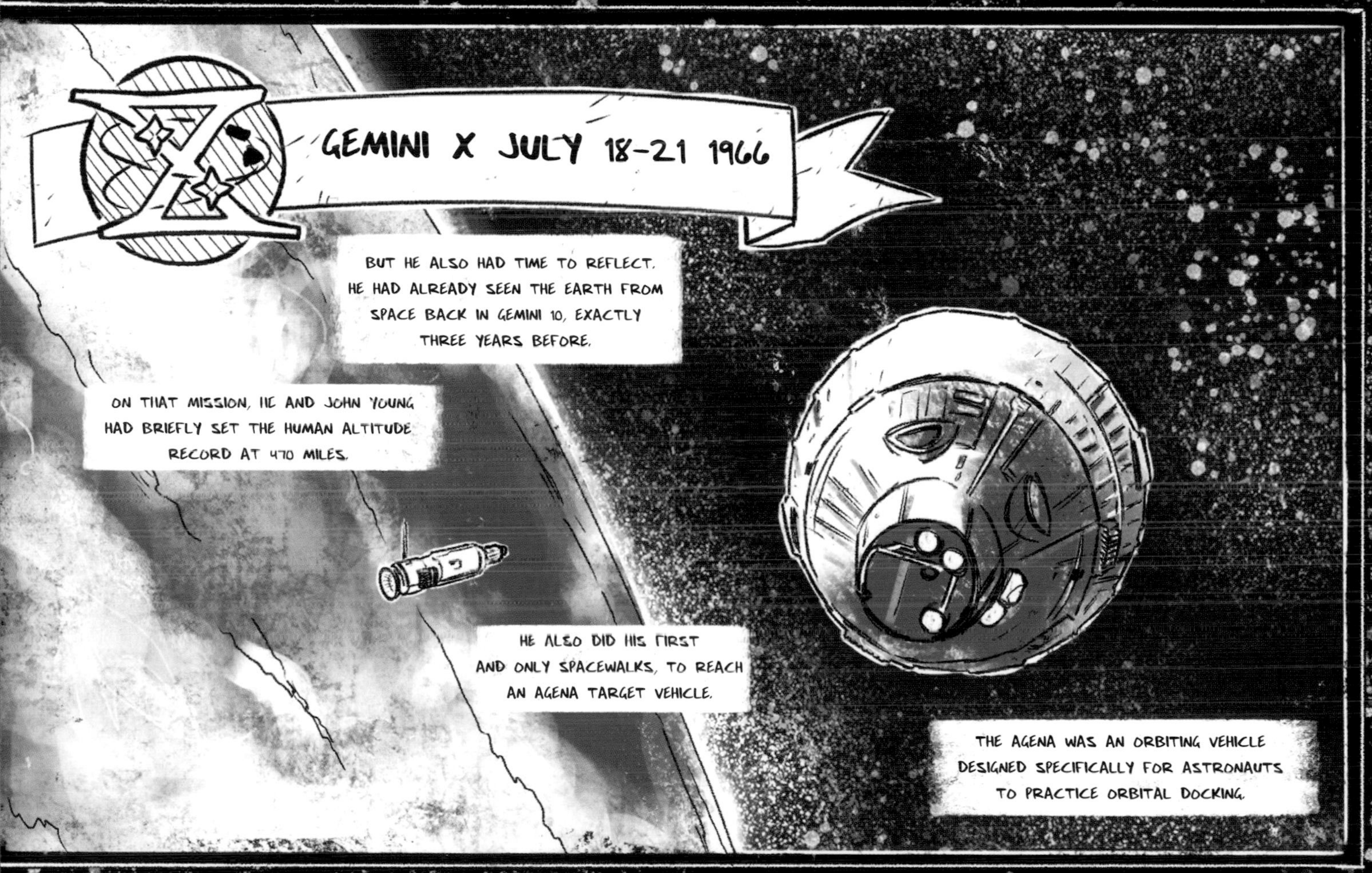
X
GEMINI X JULY 18-21 1966
BUT HE ALSO HAD TIME TO REFLECT. HE HAD ALREADY SEEN THE EARTH FROM SPACE BACK IN GEMINI 10, EXACTLY THREE YEARS BEFORE.
ON THAT MISSION, HE AND JOHN YOUNG HAD BRIEFLY SET THE HUMAN ALTITUDE RECORD AT 470 MILES.
HE ALSO DID HIS FIRST AND ONLY SPACEWALKS, TO REACH AN AGENA TARGET VEHICLE.
THE AGENA WAS AN ORBITING VEHICLE DESIGNED SPECIFICALLY FOR ASTRONAUTS TO PRACTICE ORBITAL DOCKING.

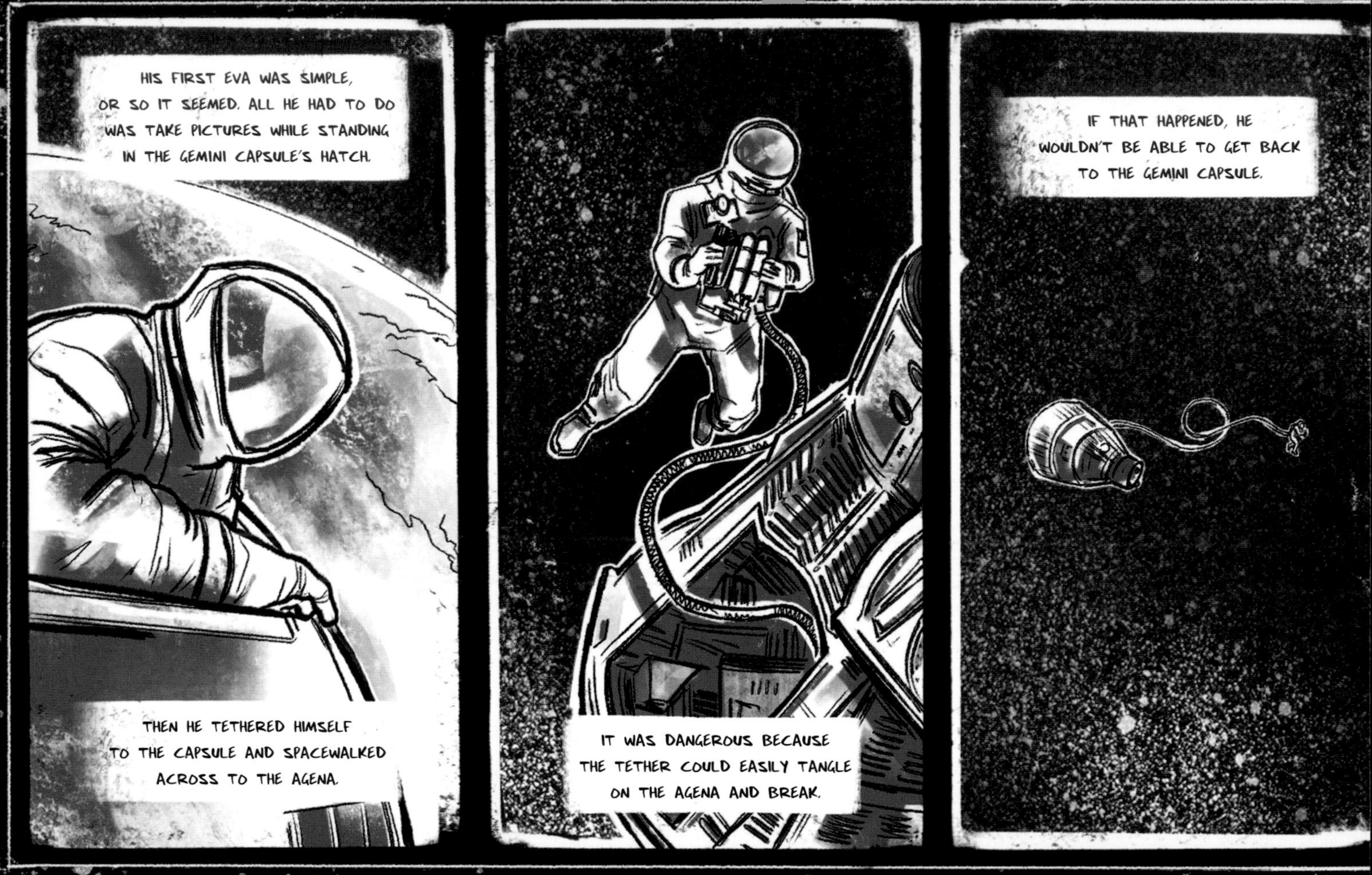
HIS FIRST EVA WAS SIMPLE, OR SO IT SEEMED. ALL HE HAD TO DO WAS TAKE PICTURES WHILE STANDING IN THE GEMINI CAPSULE'S HATCH.
THEN HE TETHERED HIMSELF TO THE CAPSULE AND SPACEWALKED ACROSS TO THE AGENA.
IT WAS DANGEROUS BECAUSE THE TETHER COULD EASILY TANGLE ON THE AGENA AND BREAK.
IF THAT HAPPENED, HE WOULDN'T BE ABLE TO GET BACK TO THE GEMINI CAPSULE.

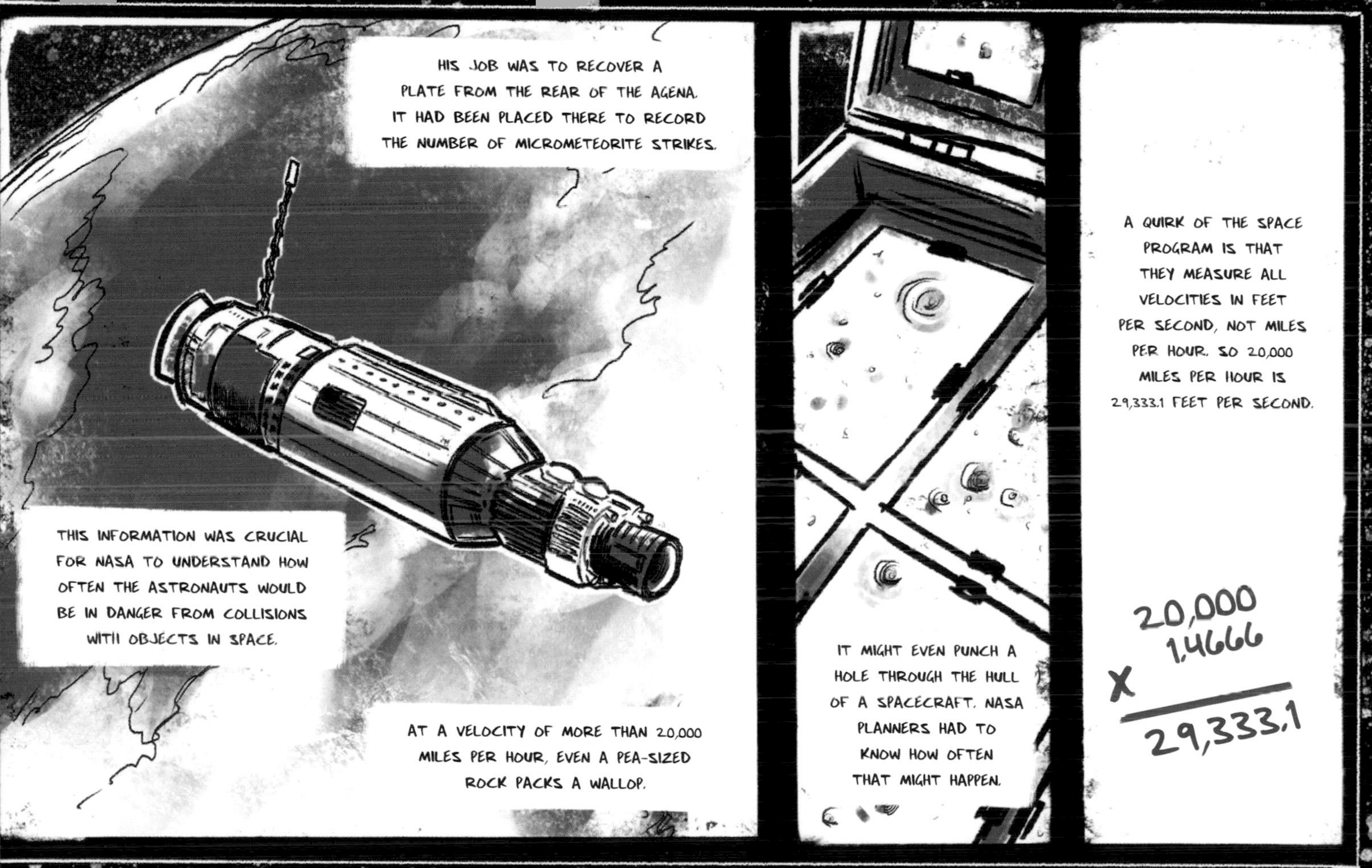

HIS JOB WAS TO RECOVER A PLATE FROM THE REAR OF THE AGENA. IT HAD BEEN PLACED THERE TO RECORD THE NUMBER OF MICROMETEORITE STRIKES.

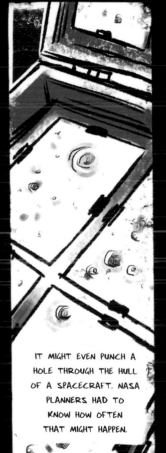

THIS INFORMATION WAS CRUCIAL FOR NASA TO UNDERSTAND HOW OFTEN THE ASTRONAUTS WOULD BE IN DANGER FROM COLLISIONS WITH OBJECTS IN SPACE.

AT A VELOCITY OF MORE THAN 20,000 MILES PER HOUR, EVEN A PEA-SIZED ROCK PACKS A WALLOP.

IT MIGHT EVEN PUNCH A HOLE THROUGH THE HULL OF A SPACECRAFT. NASA PLANNERS HAD TO KNOW HOW OFTEN THAT MIGHT HAPPEN.

A QUIRK OF THE SPACE PROGRAM IS THAT THEY MEASURE ALL VELOCITIES IN FEET PER SECOND, NOT MILES PER HOUR. SO 20,000 MILES PER HOUR IS 29,333.1 FEET PER SECOND.

$$\begin{array}{r} 20{,}000 \\ \times\ 1.4666 \\ \hline 29{,}333.1 \end{array}$$

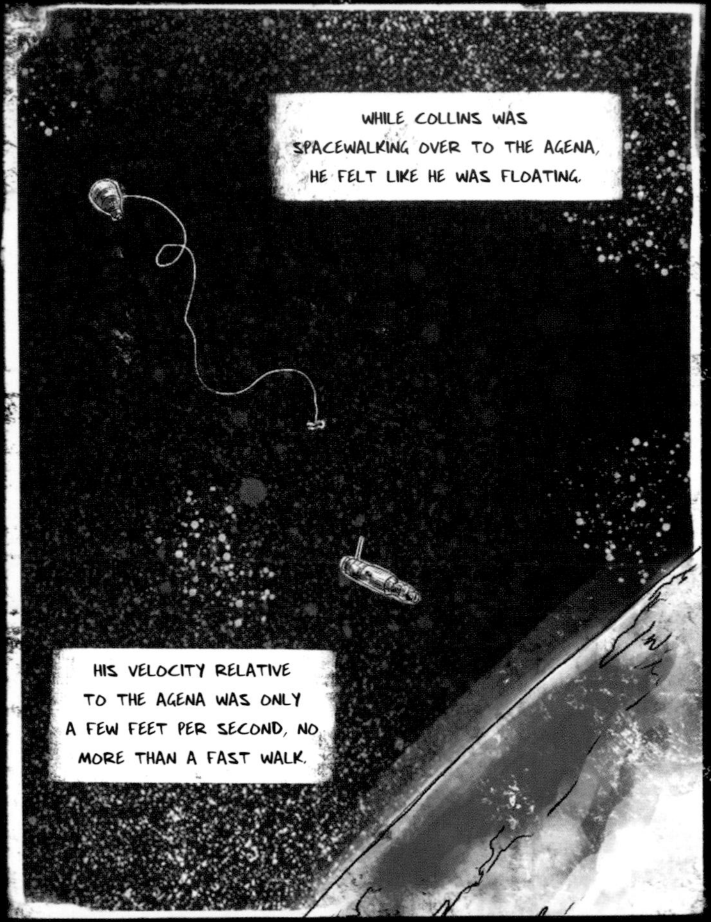
WHILE COLLINS WAS SPACEWALKING OVER TO THE AGENA, HE FELT LIKE HE WAS FLOATING.
HIS VELOCITY RELATIVE TO THE AGENA WAS ONLY A FEW FEET PER SECOND, NO MORE THAN A FAST WALK.

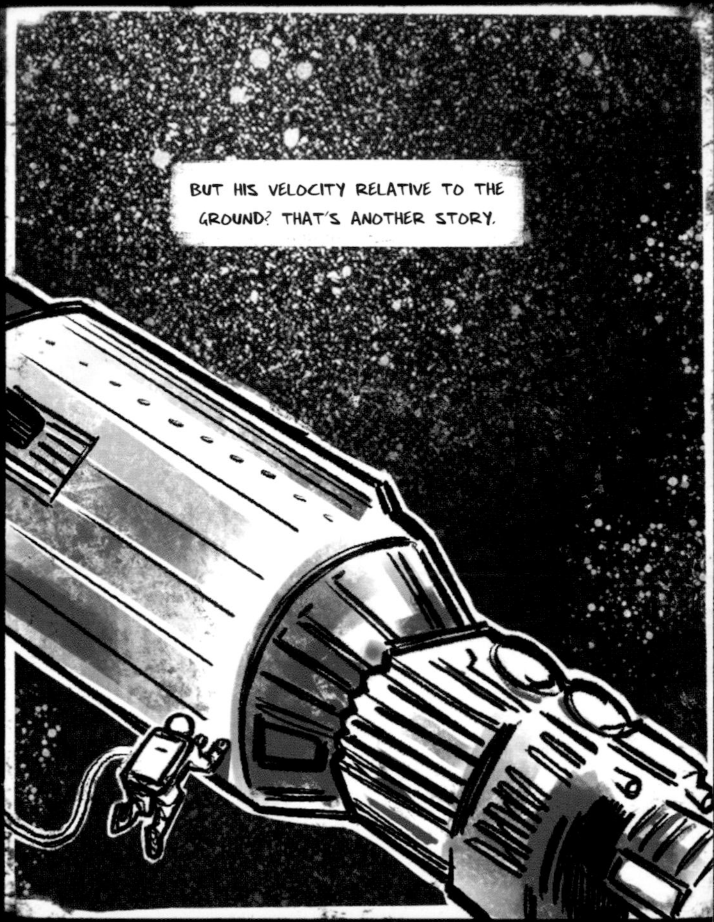
BUT HIS VELOCITY RELATIVE TO THE GROUND? THAT'S ANOTHER STORY.

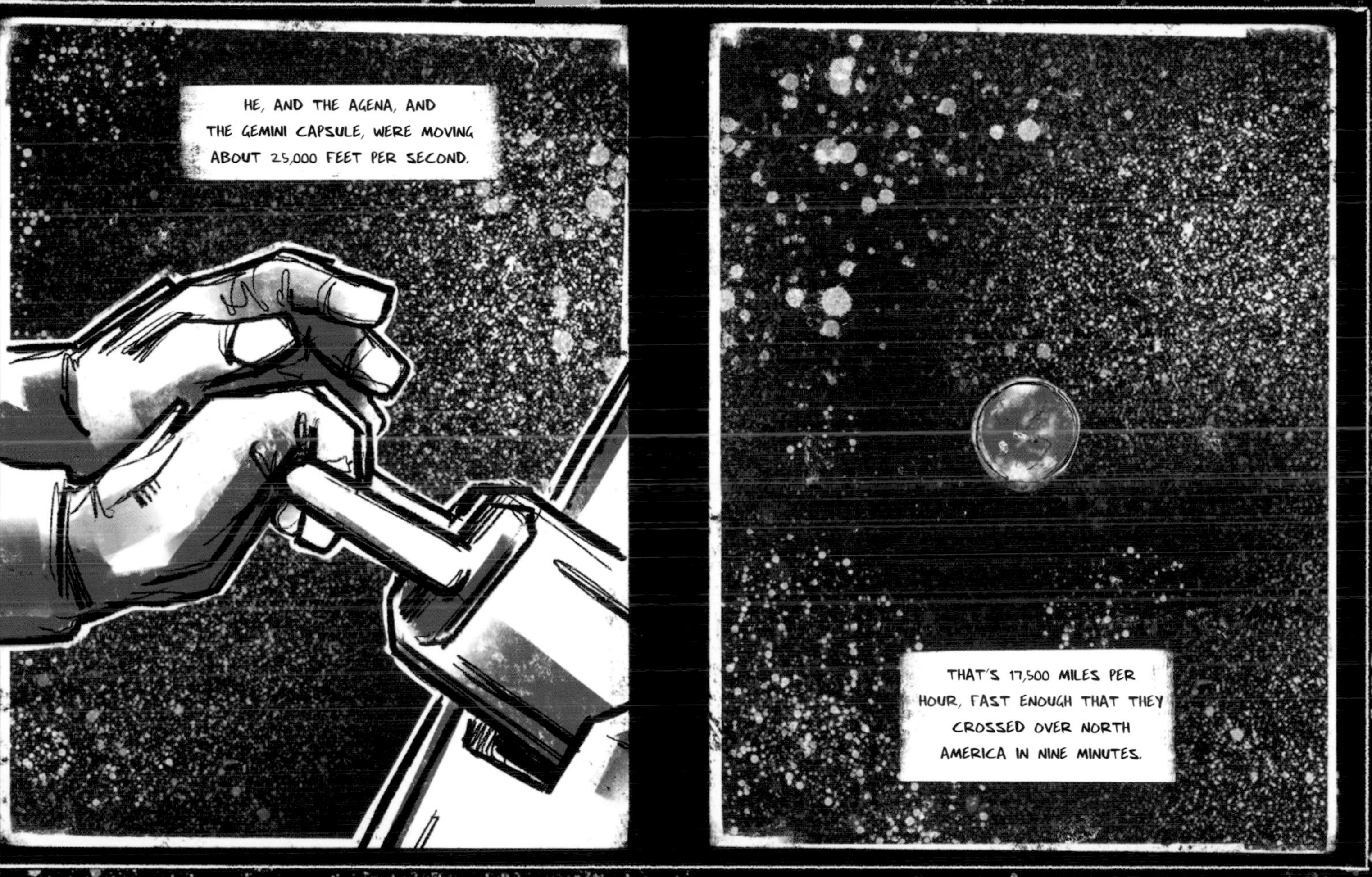
HE, AND THE AGENA, AND THE GEMINI CAPSULE, WERE MOVING ABOUT 25,000 FEET PER SECOND.
THAT'S 17,500 MILES PER HOUR, FAST ENOUGH THAT THEY CROSSED OVER NORTH AMERICA IN NINE MINUTES.

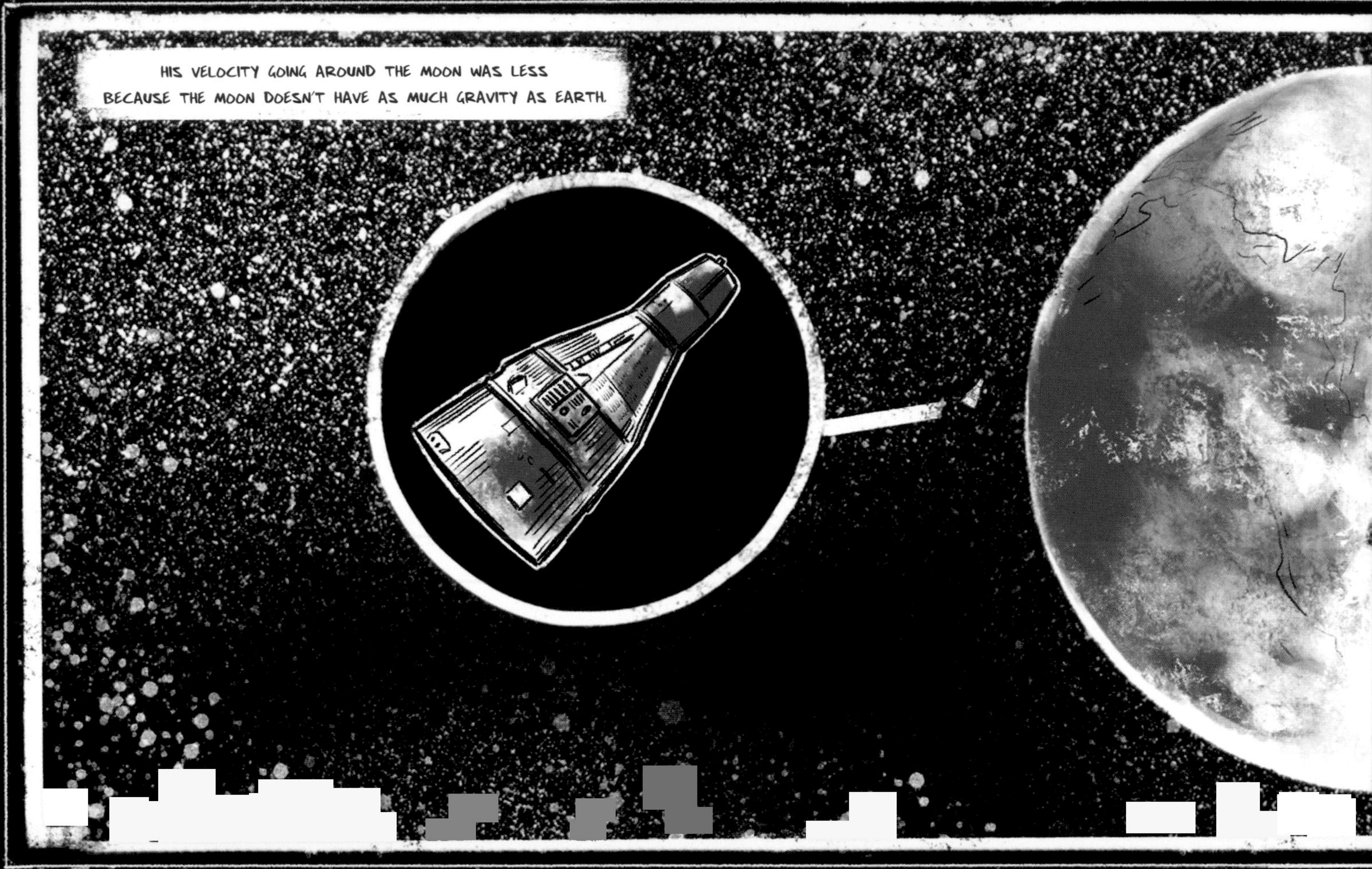
HIS VELOCITY GOING AROUND THE MOON WAS LESS BECAUSE THE MOON DOESN'T HAVE AS MUCH GRAVITY AS EARTH.

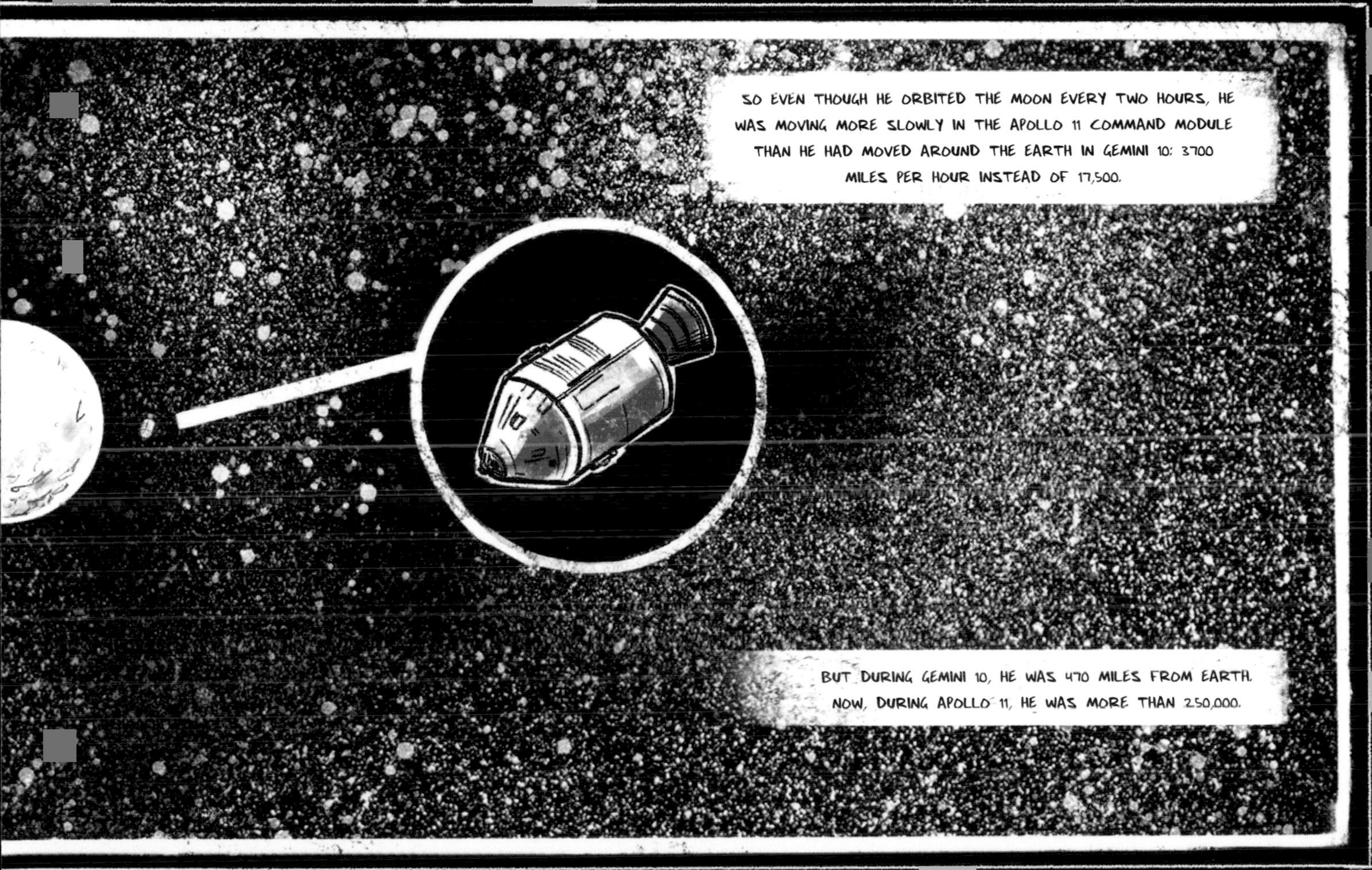
SO EVEN THOUGH HE ORBITED THE MOON EVERY TWO HOURS, HE WAS MOVING MORE SLOWLY IN THE APOLLO 11 COMMAND MODULE THAN HE HAD MOVED AROUND THE EARTH IN GEMINI 10: 3700 MILES PER HOUR INSTEAD OF 17,500.
BUT DURING GEMINI 10, HE WAS 470 MILES FROM EARTH. NOW, DURING APOLLO 11, HE WAS MORE THAN 250,000.

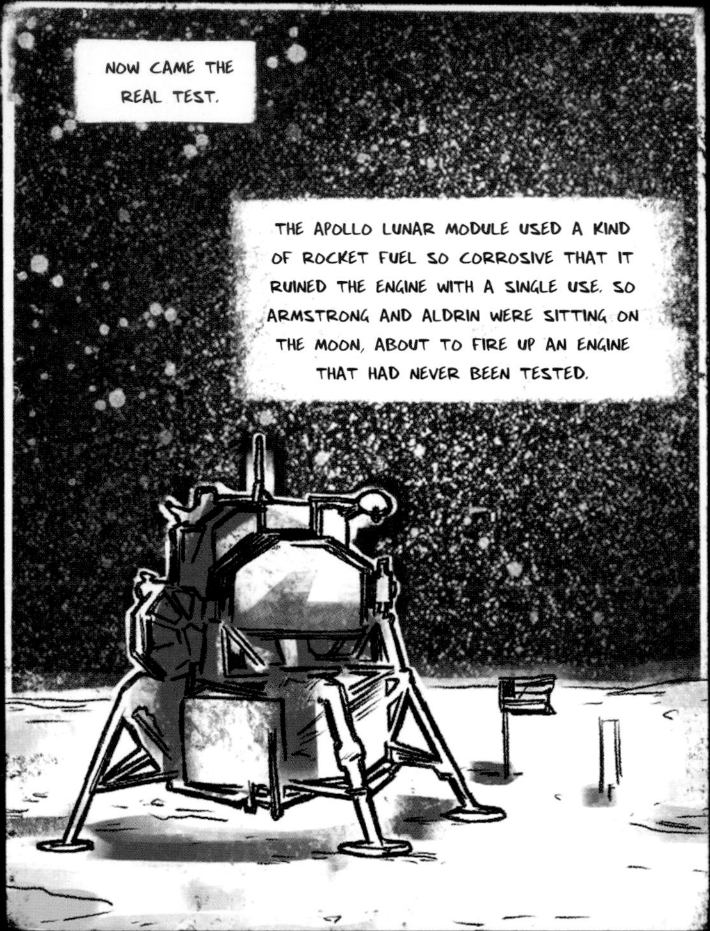
NOW CAME THE REAL TEST.
THE APOLLO LUNAR MODULE USED A KIND OF ROCKET FUEL SO CORROSIVE THAT IT RUINED THE ENGINE WITH A SINGLE USE. SO ARMSTRONG AND ALDRIN WERE SITTING ON THE MOON, ABOUT TO FIRE UP AN ENGINE THAT HAD NEVER BEEN TESTED.

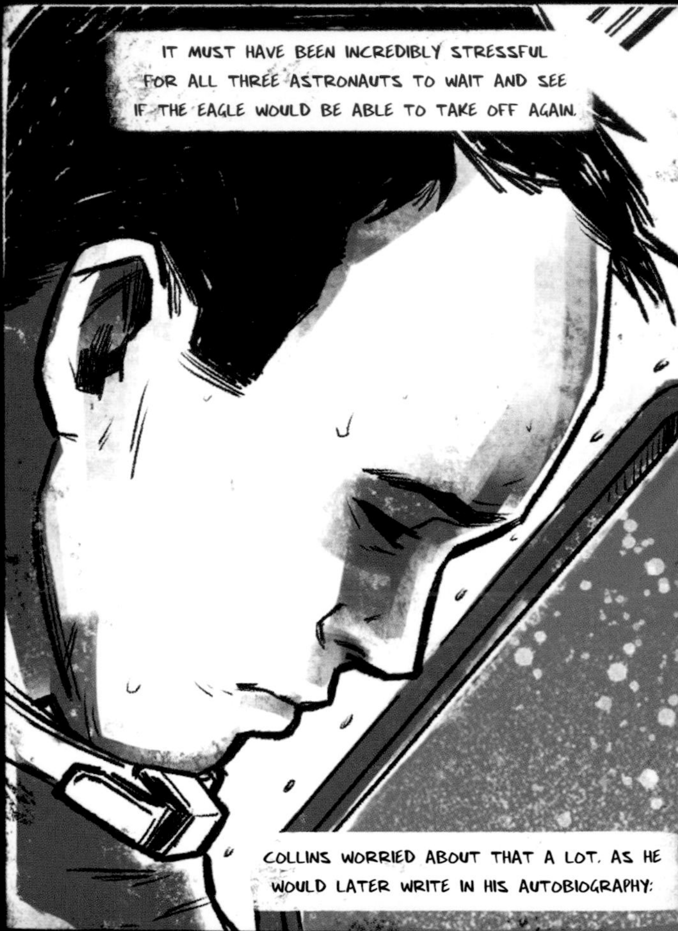
IT MUST HAVE BEEN INCREDIBLY STRESSFUL FOR ALL THREE ASTRONAUTS TO WAIT AND SEE IF THE EAGLE WOULD BE ABLE TO TAKE OFF AGAIN.
COLLINS WORRIED ABOUT THAT A LOT. AS HE WOULD LATER WRITE IN HIS AUTOBIOGRAPHY:

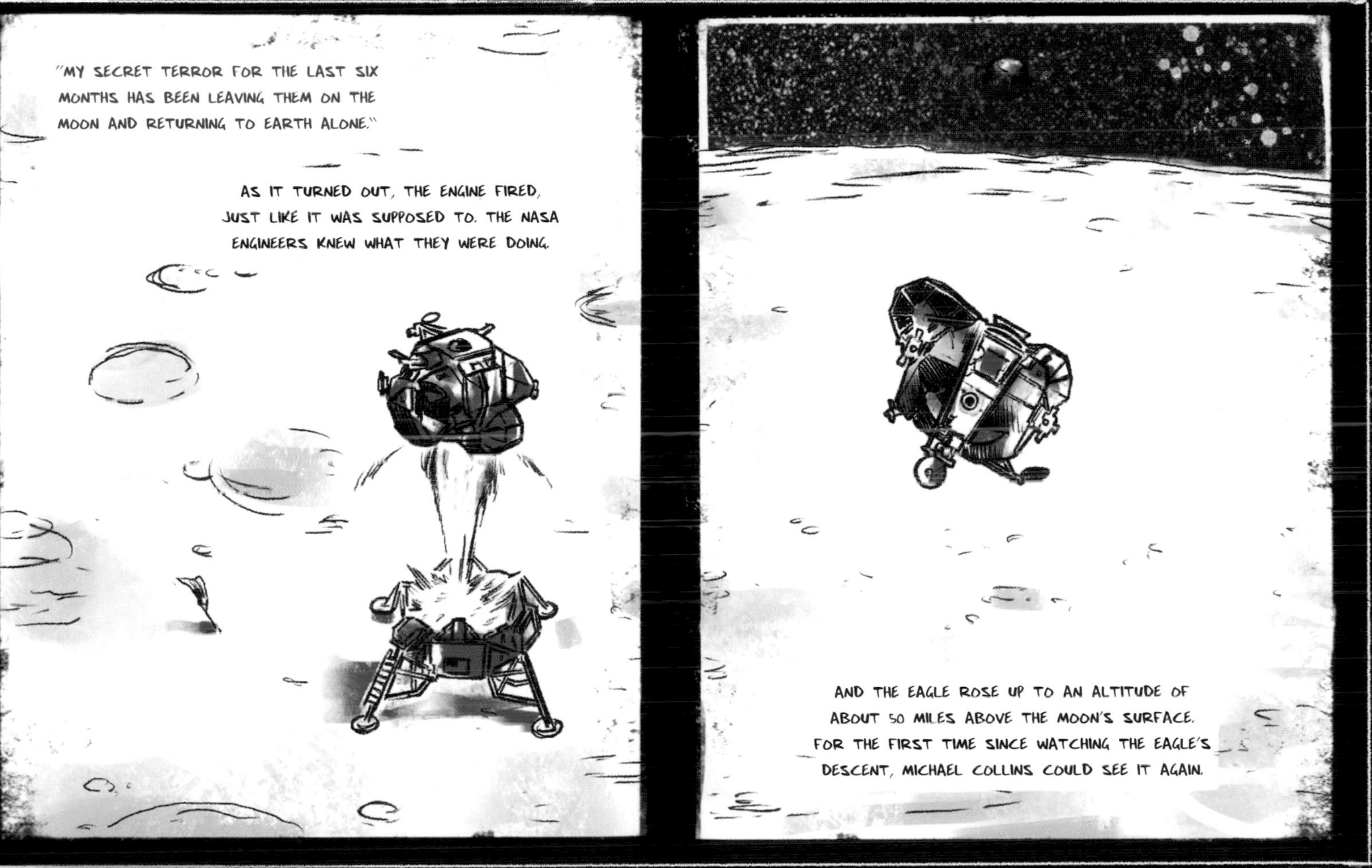
"MY SECRET TERROR FOR THE LAST SIX MONTHS HAS BEEN LEAVING THEM ON THE MOON AND RETURNING TO EARTH ALONE."
AS IT TURNED OUT, THE ENGINE FIRED, JUST LIKE IT WAS SUPPOSED TO. THE NASA ENGINEERS KNEW WHAT THEY WERE DOING.
AND THE EAGLE ROSE UP TO AN ALTITUDE OF ABOUT 50 MILES ABOVE THE MOON'S SURFACE. FOR THE FIRST TIME SINCE WATCHING THE EAGLE'S DESCENT, MICHAEL COLLINS COULD SEE IT AGAIN.

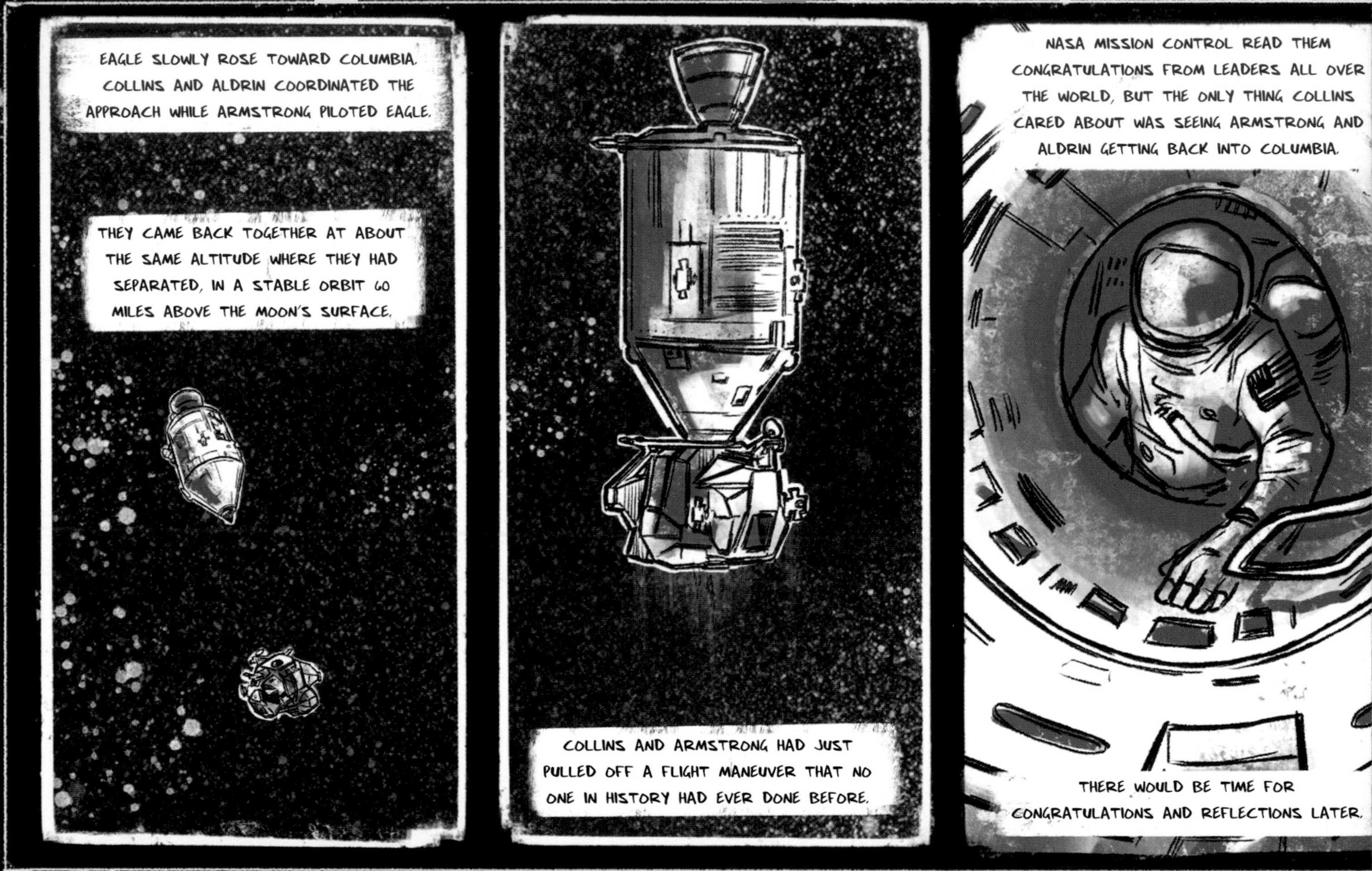
EAGLE SLOWLY ROSE TOWARD COLUMBIA. COLLINS AND ALDRIN COORDINATED THE APPROACH WHILE ARMSTRONG PILOTED EAGLE.
THEY CAME BACK TOGETHER AT ABOUT THE SAME ALTITUDE WHERE THEY HAD SEPARATED, IN A STABLE ORBIT 60 MILES ABOVE THE MOON'S SURFACE.
COLLINS AND ARMSTRONG HAD JUST PULLED OFF A FLIGHT MANEUVER THAT NO ONE IN HISTORY HAD EVER DONE BEFORE.
NASA MISSION CONTROL READ THEM CONGRATULATIONS FROM LEADERS ALL OVER THE WORLD, BUT THE ONLY THING COLLINS CARED ABOUT WAS SEEING ARMSTRONG AND ALDRIN GETTING BACK INTO COLUMBIA.
THERE WOULD BE TIME FOR CONGRATULATIONS AND REFLECTIONS LATER.

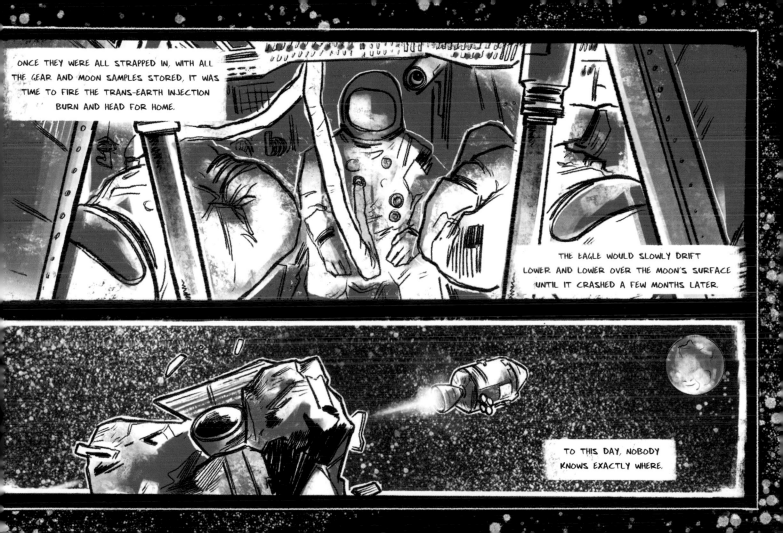

ONCE THEY WERE ALL STRAPPED IN, WITH ALL THE GEAR AND MOON SAMPLES STORED, IT WAS TIME TO FIRE THE TRANS-EARTH INJECTION BURN AND HEAD FOR HOME.

THE EAGLE WOULD SLOWLY DRIFT LOWER AND LOWER OVER THE MOON'S SURFACE UNTIL IT CRASHED A FEW MONTHS LATER.

TO THIS DAY, NOBODY KNOWS EXACTLY WHERE.

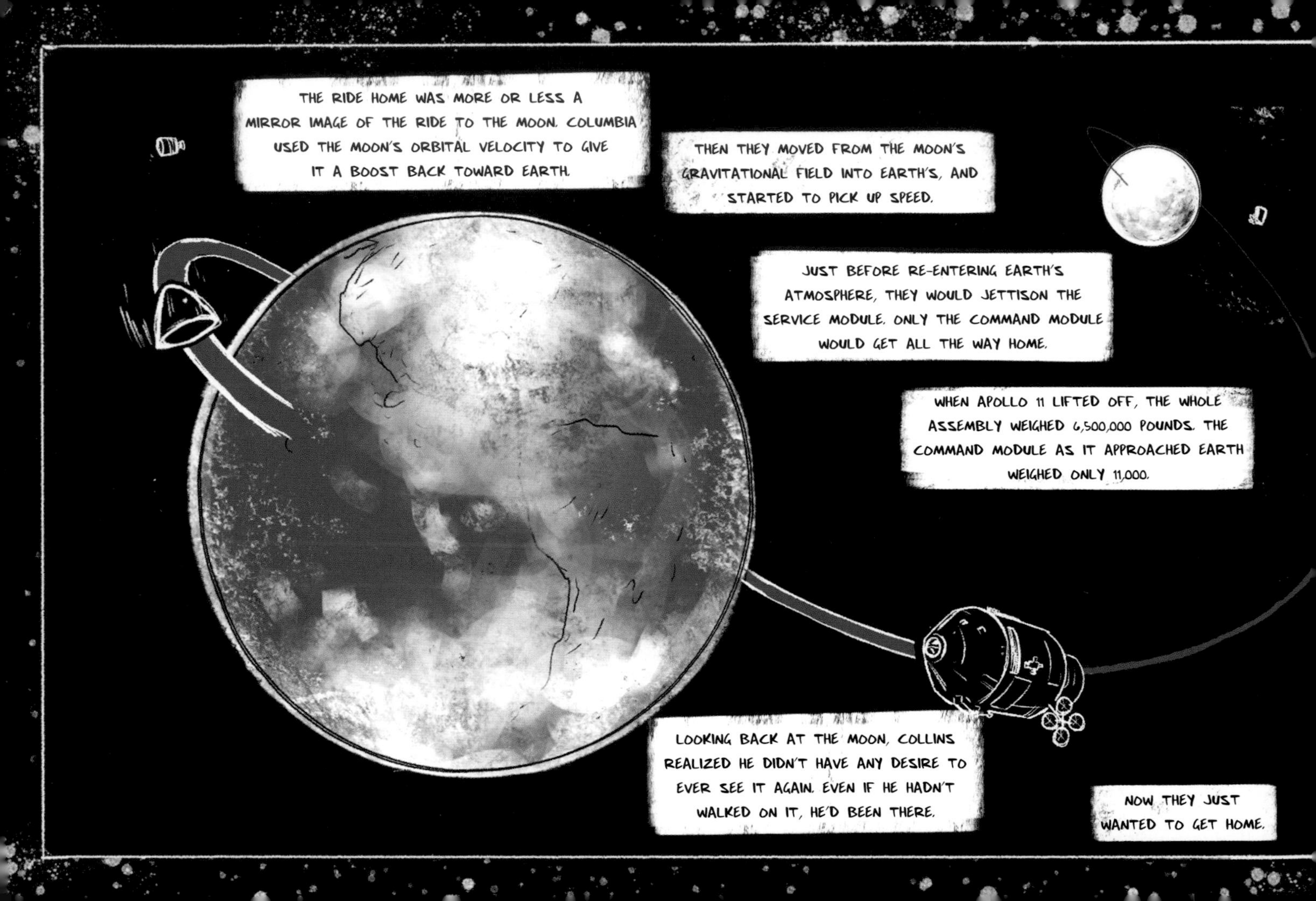
THE RIDE HOME WAS MORE OR LESS A MIRROR IMAGE OF THE RIDE TO THE MOON. COLUMBIA USED THE MOON'S ORBITAL VELOCITY TO GIVE IT A BOOST BACK TOWARD EARTH.
THEN THEY MOVED FROM THE MOON'S GRAVITATIONAL FIELD INTO EARTH'S, AND STARTED TO PICK UP SPEED.
JUST BEFORE RE-ENTERING EARTH'S ATMOSPHERE, THEY WOULD JETTISON THE SERVICE MODULE. ONLY THE COMMAND MODULE WOULD GET ALL THE WAY HOME.
WHEN APOLLO 11 LIFTED OFF, THE WHOLE ASSEMBLY WEIGHED 6,500,000 POUNDS. THE COMMAND MODULE AS IT APPROACHED EARTH WEIGHED ONLY 11,000.
LOOKING BACK AT THE MOON, COLLINS REALIZED HE DIDN'T HAVE ANY DESIRE TO EVER SEE IT AGAIN. EVEN IF HE HADN'T WALKED ON IT, HE'D BEEN THERE.
NOW THEY JUST WANTED TO GET HOME.

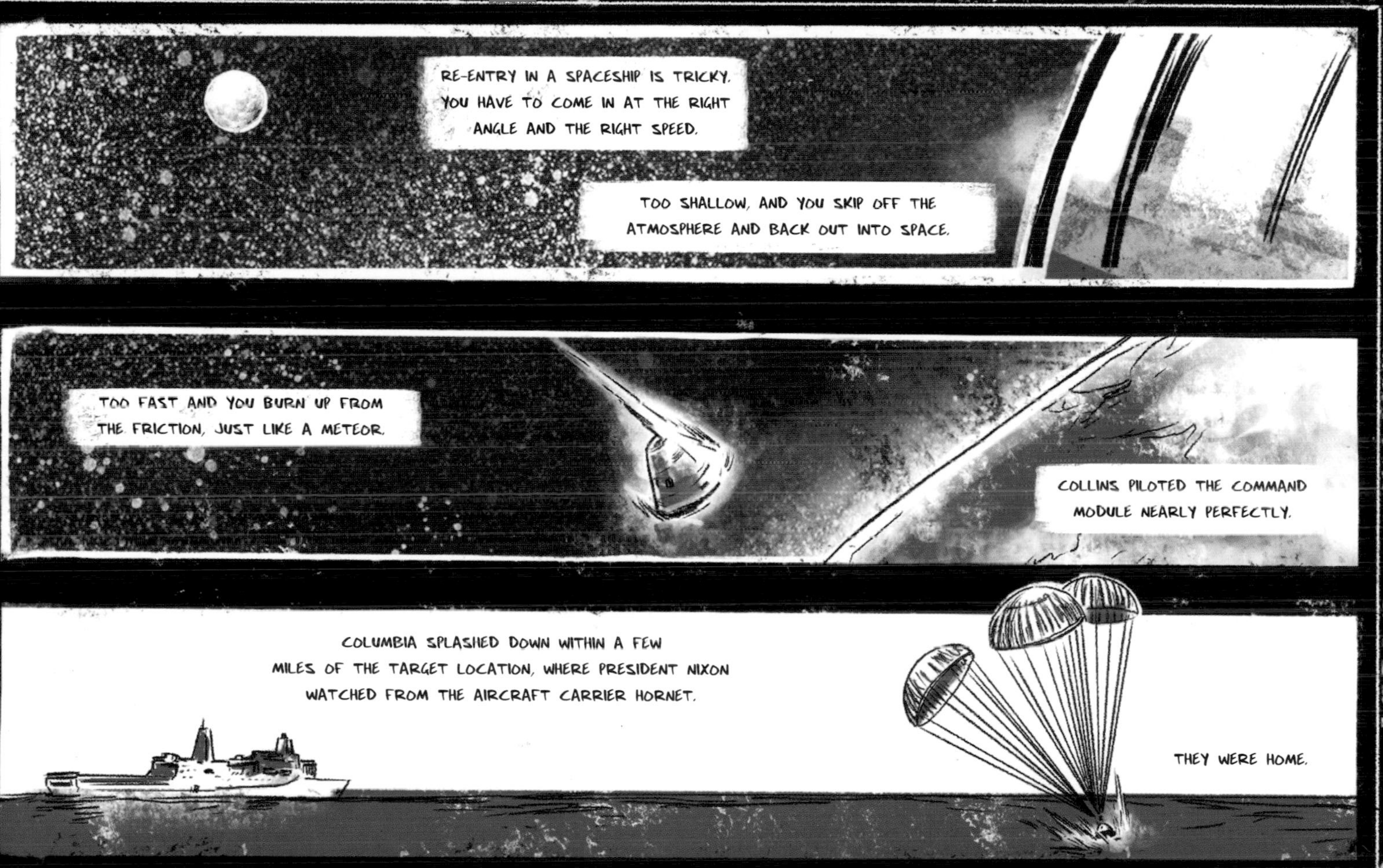
RE-ENTRY IN A SPACESHIP IS TRICKY. YOU HAVE TO COME IN AT THE RIGHT ANGLE AND THE RIGHT SPEED.
TOO SHALLOW, AND YOU SKIP OFF THE ATMOSPHERE AND BACK OUT INTO SPACE.
TOO FAST AND YOU BURN UP FROM THE FRICTION, JUST LIKE A METEOR.
COLLINS PILOTED THE COMMAND MODULE NEARLY PERFECTLY.
COLUMBIA SPLASHED DOWN WITHIN A FEW MILES OF THE TARGET LOCATION, WHERE PRESIDENT NIXON WATCHED FROM THE AIRCRAFT CARRIER HORNET.
THEY WERE HOME.

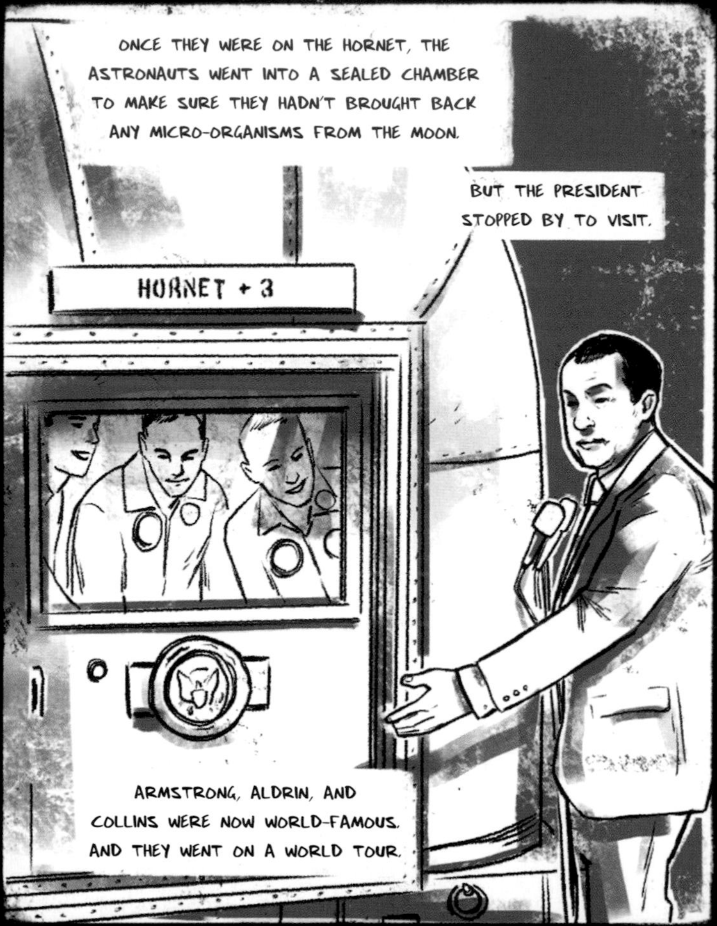
ONCE THEY WERE ON THE HORNET, THE ASTRONAUTS WENT INTO A SEALED CHAMBER TO MAKE SURE THEY HADN'T BROUGHT BACK ANY MICRO-ORGANISMS FROM THE MOON.
BUT THE PRESIDENT STOPPED BY TO VISIT.
HORNET + 3
ARMSTRONG, ALDRIN, AND COLLINS WERE NOW WORLD-FAMOUS. AND THEY WENT ON A WORLD TOUR.

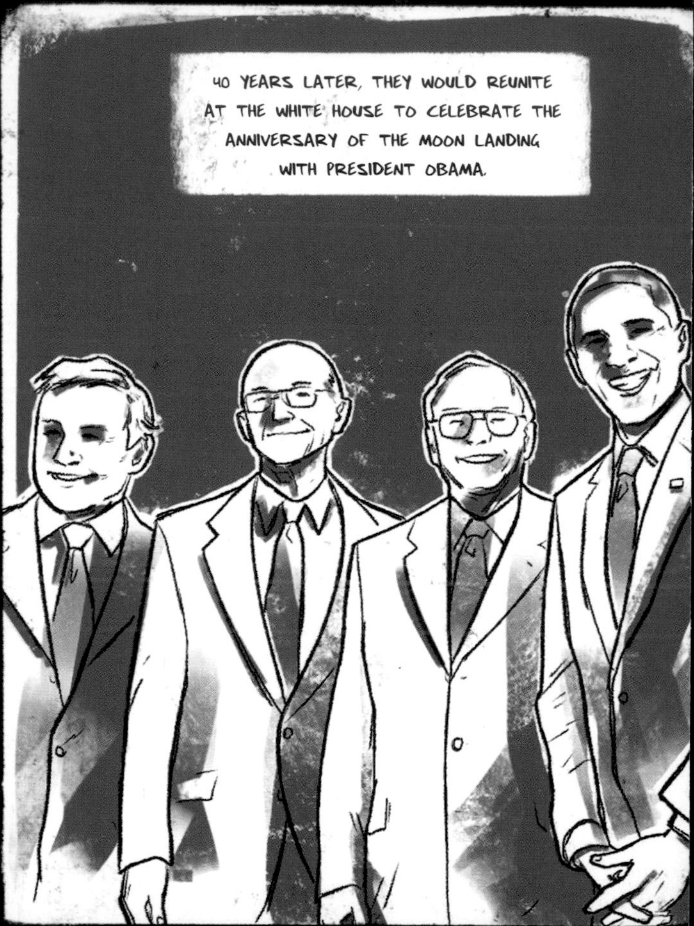
40 YEARS LATER, THEY WOULD REUNITE AT THE WHITE HOUSE TO CELEBRATE THE ANNIVERSARY OF THE MOON LANDING WITH PRESIDENT OBAMA.

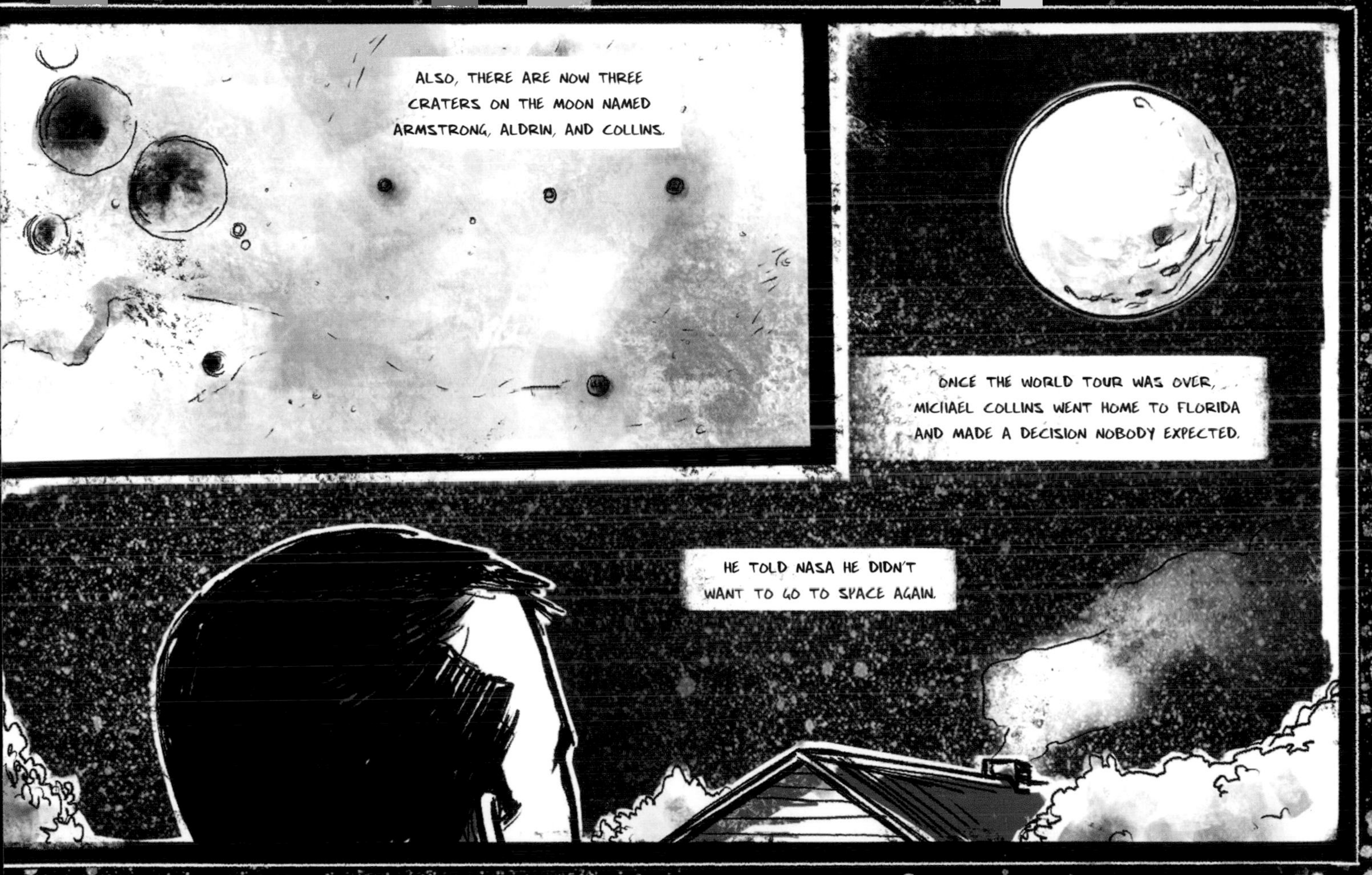
ALSO, THERE ARE NOW THREE CRATERS ON THE MOON NAMED ARMSTRONG, ALDRIN, AND COLLINS.
ONCE THE WORLD TOUR WAS OVER, MICHAEL COLLINS WENT HOME TO FLORIDA AND MADE A DECISION NOBODY EXPECTED.
HE TOLD NASA HE DIDN'T WANT TO GO TO SPACE AGAIN.

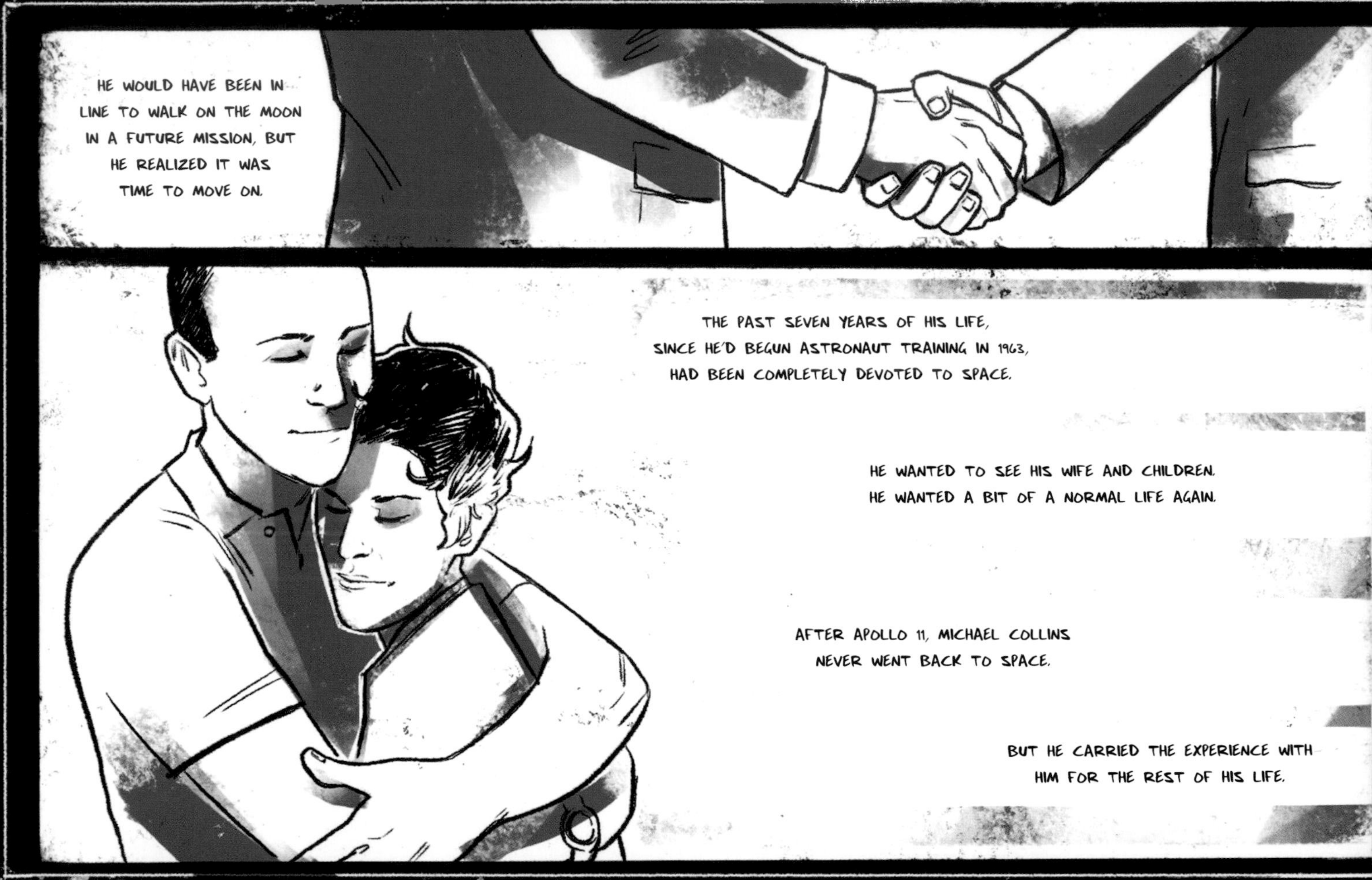
HE WOULD HAVE BEEN IN LINE TO WALK ON THE MOON IN A FUTURE MISSION, BUT HE REALIZED IT WAS TIME TO MOVE ON.
THE PAST SEVEN YEARS OF HIS LIFE, SINCE HE'D BEGUN ASTRONAUT TRAINING IN 1963, HAD BEEN COMPLETELY DEVOTED TO SPACE.
HE WANTED TO SEE HIS WIFE AND CHILDREN. HE WANTED A BIT OF A NORMAL LIFE AGAIN.
AFTER APOLLO 11, MICHAEL COLLINS NEVER WENT BACK TO SPACE.
BUT HE CARRIED THE EXPERIENCE WITH HIM FOR THE REST OF HIS LIFE.

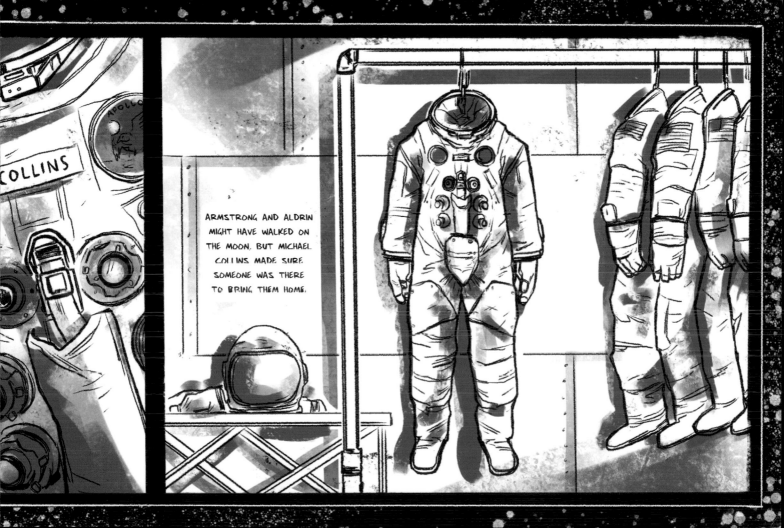

ARMSTRONG AND ALDRIN MIGHT HAVE WALKED ON THE MOON, BUT MICHAEL COLLINS MADE SURE SOMEONE WAS THERE TO BRING THEM HOME.

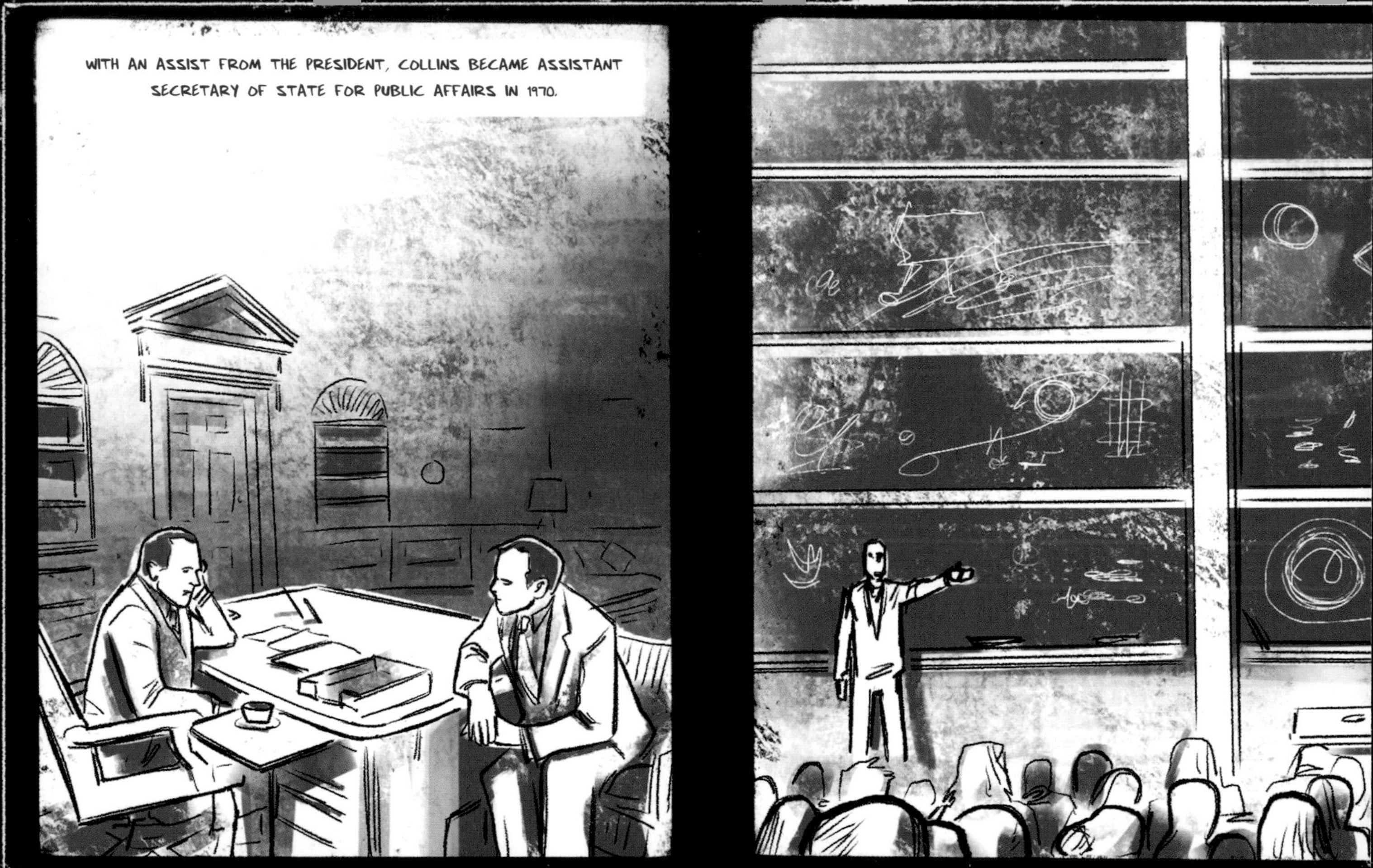
WITH AN ASSIST FROM THE PRESIDENT, COLLINS BECAME ASSISTANT SECRETARY OF STATE FOR PUBLIC AFFAIRS IN 1970.

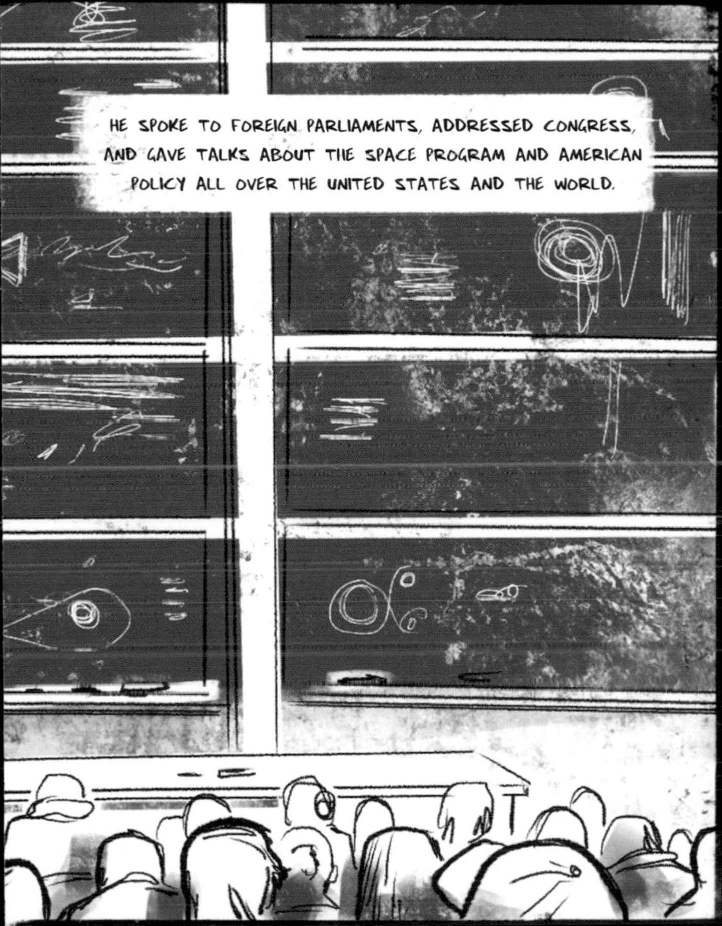
HE SPOKE TO FOREIGN PARLIAMENTS, ADDRESSED CONGRESS, AND GAVE TALKS ABOUT THE SPACE PROGRAM AND AMERICAN POLICY ALL OVER THE UNITED STATES AND THE WORLD.

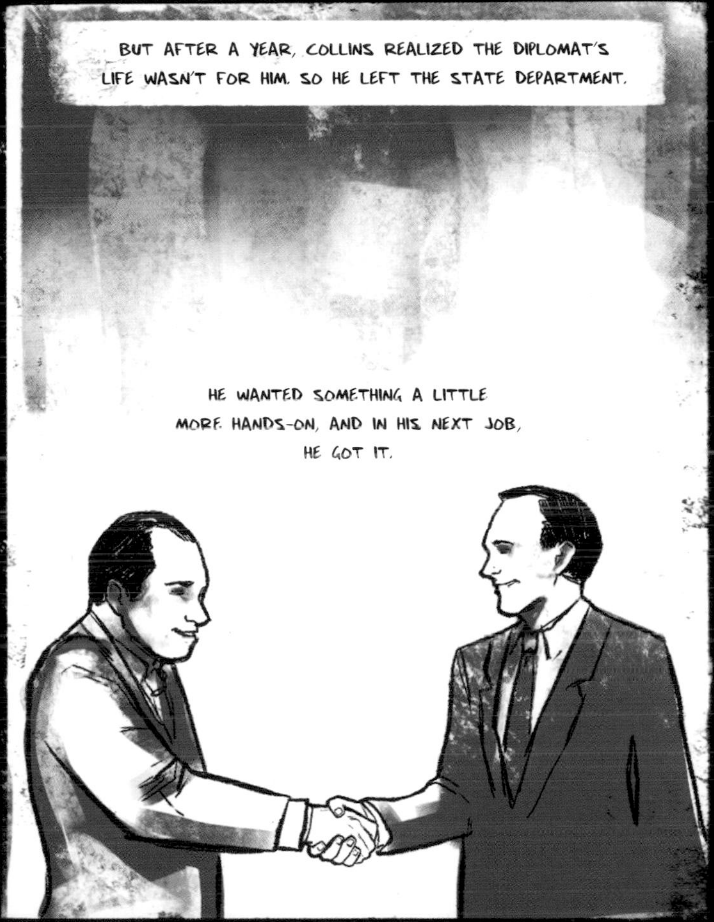
BUT AFTER A YEAR, COLLINS REALIZED THE DIPLOMAT'S LIFE WASN'T FOR HIM, SO HE LEFT THE STATE DEPARTMENT.
HE WANTED SOMETHING A LITTLE MORE HANDS-ON, AND IN HIS NEXT JOB, HE GOT IT.

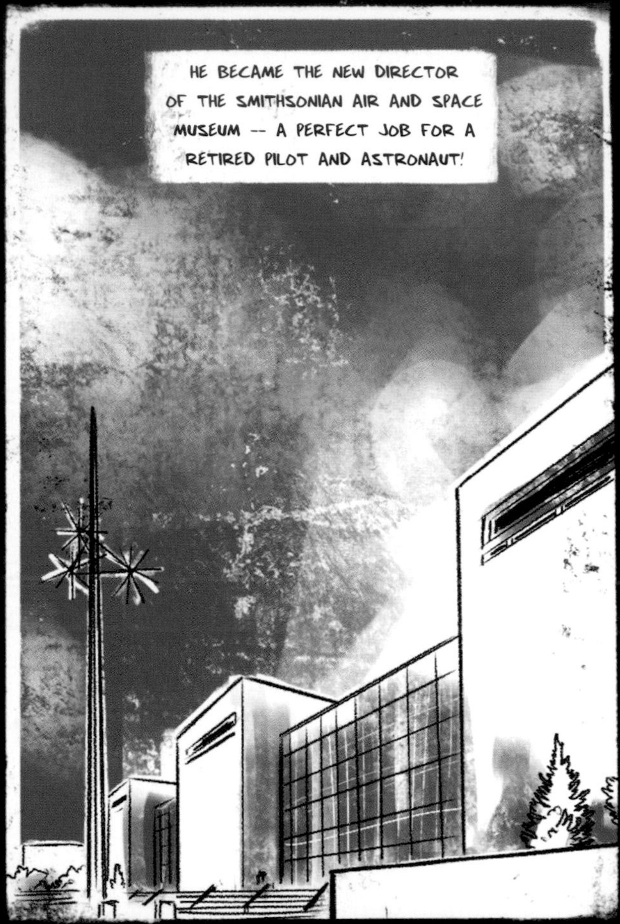
HE BECAME THE NEW DIRECTOR OF THE SMITHSONIAN AIR AND SPACE MUSEUM -- A PERFECT JOB FOR A RETIRED PILOT AND ASTRONAUT!

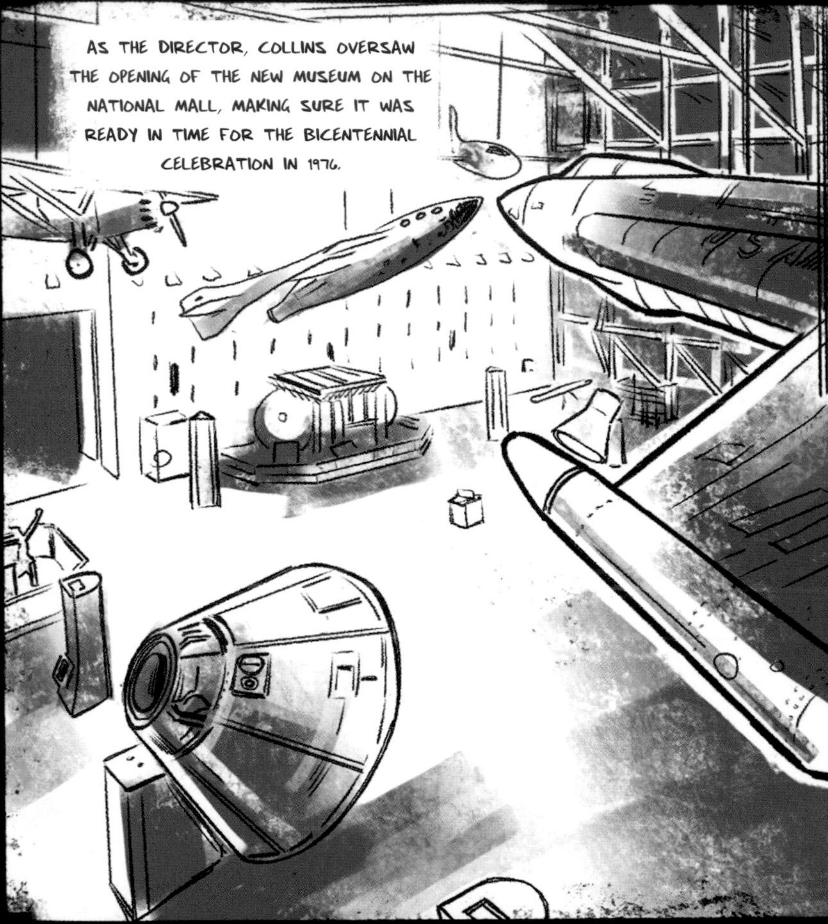
AS THE DIRECTOR, COLLINS OVERSAW THE OPENING OF THE NEW MUSEUM ON THE NATIONAL MALL, MAKING SURE IT WAS READY IN TIME FOR THE BICENTENNIAL CELEBRATION IN 1976.

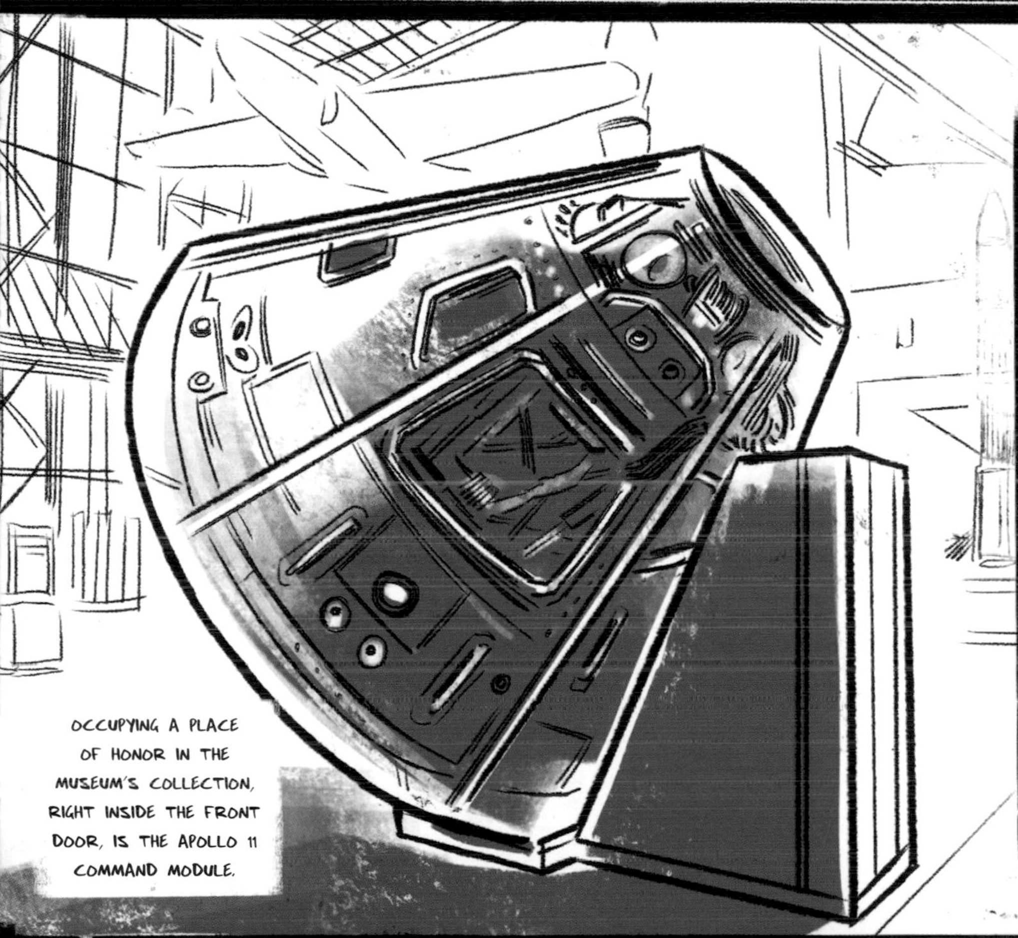
OCCUPYING A PLACE OF HONOR IN THE MUSEUM'S COLLECTION, RIGHT INSIDE THE FRONT DOOR, IS THE APOLLO 11 COMMAND MODULE.

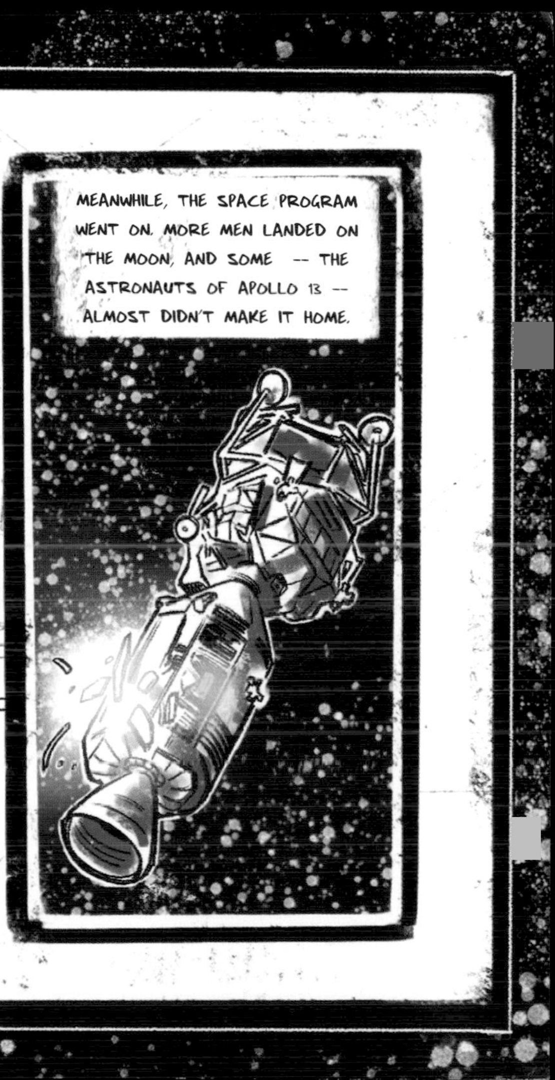
MEANWHILE, THE SPACE PROGRAM WENT ON. MORE MEN LANDED ON THE MOON, AND SOME -- THE ASTRONAUTS OF APOLLO 13 -- ALMOST DIDN'T MAKE IT HOME.

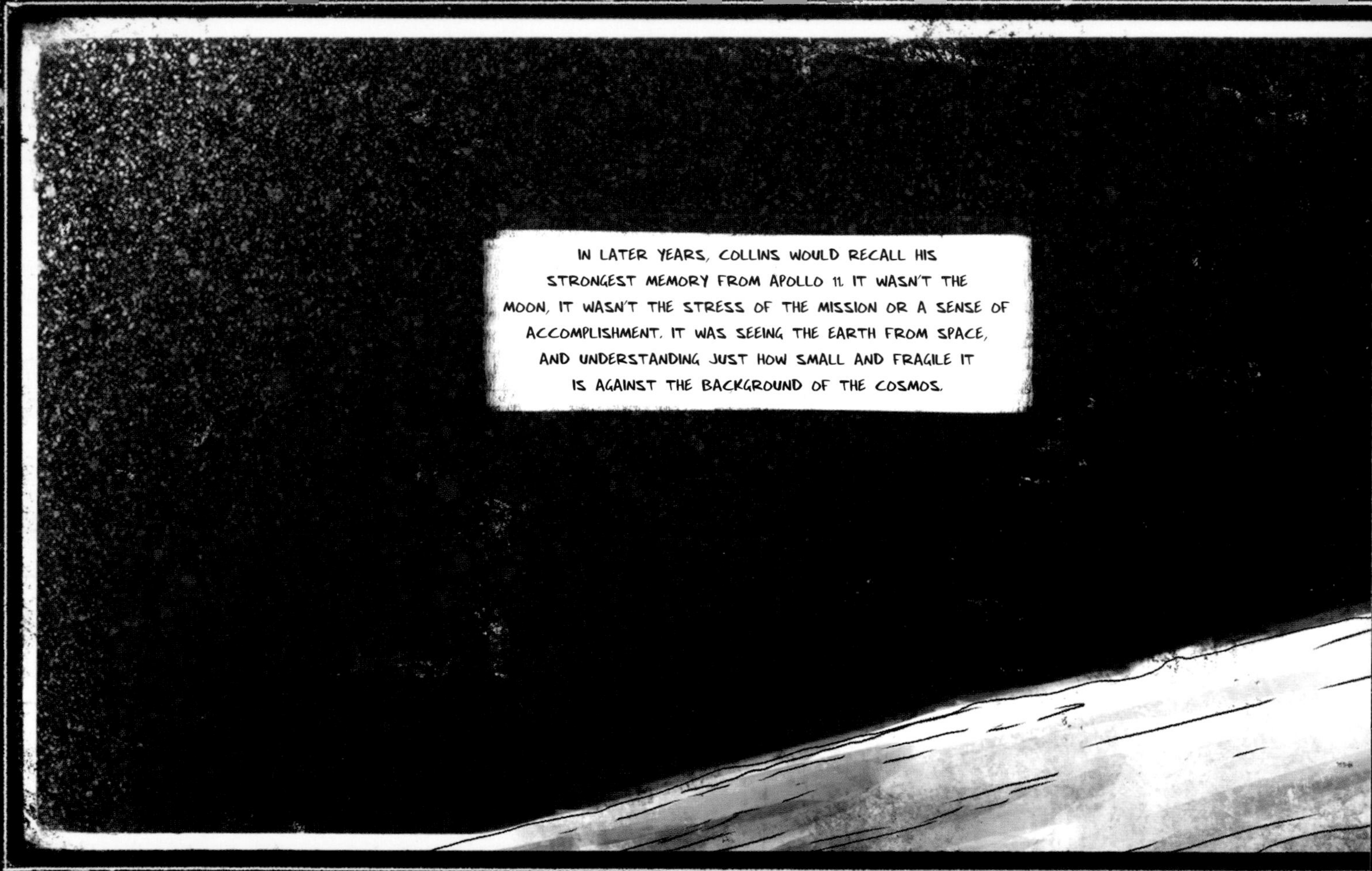
IN LATER YEARS, COLLINS WOULD RECALL HIS STRONGEST MEMORY FROM APOLLO 11. IT WASN'T THE MOON, IT WASN'T THE STRESS OF THE MISSION OR A SENSE OF ACCOMPLISHMENT. IT WAS SEEING THE EARTH FROM SPACE, AND UNDERSTANDING JUST HOW SMALL AND FRAGILE IT IS AGAINST THE BACKGROUND OF THE COSMOS.

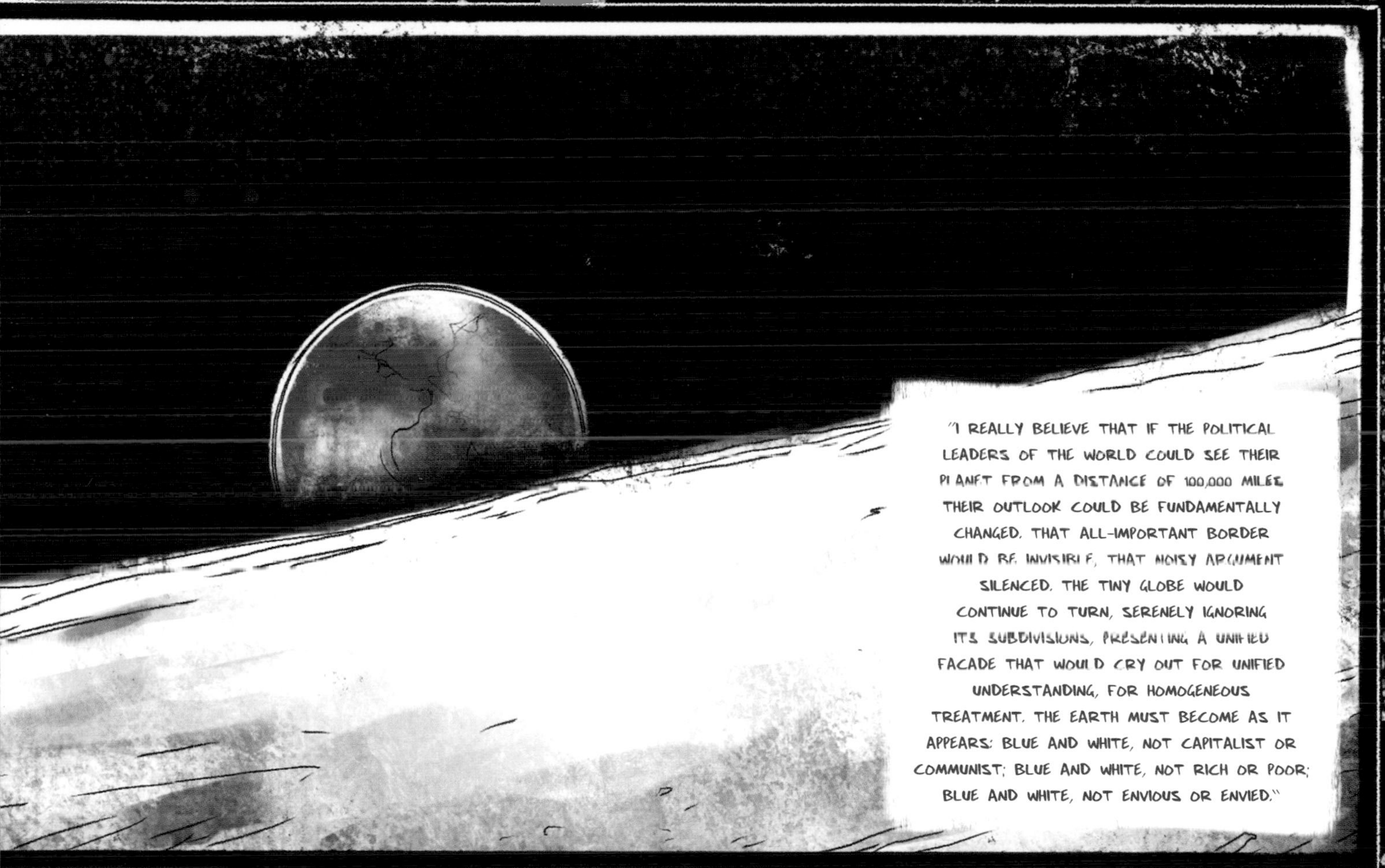
"I REALLY BELIEVE THAT IF THE POLITICAL LEADERS OF THE WORLD COULD SEE THEIR PLANET FROM A DISTANCE OF 100,000 MILES THEIR OUTLOOK COULD BE FUNDAMENTALLY CHANGED. THAT ALL-IMPORTANT BORDER WOULD BE INVISIBLE, THAT NOISY ARGUMENT SILENCED. THE TINY GLOBE WOULD CONTINUE TO TURN, SERENELY IGNORING ITS SUBDIVISIONS, PRESENTING A UNIFIED FACADE THAT WOULD CRY OUT FOR UNIFIED UNDERSTANDING, FOR HOMOGENEOUS TREATMENT. THE EARTH MUST BECOME AS IT APPEARS: BLUE AND WHITE, NOT CAPITALIST OR COMMUNIST; BLUE AND WHITE, NOT RICH OR POOR; BLUE AND WHITE, NOT ENVIOUS OR ENVIED."

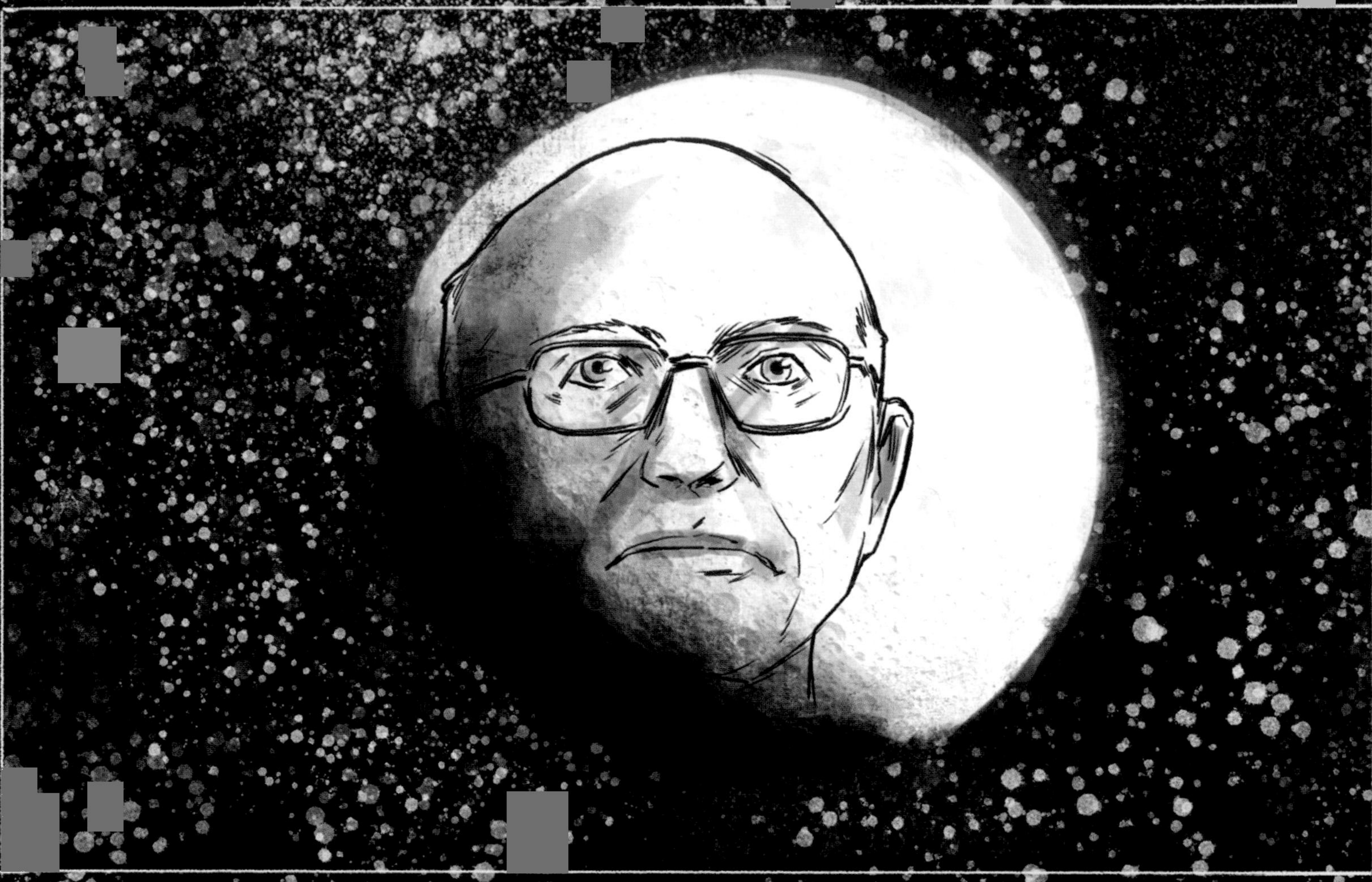

THAT'S THE STORY OF
MICHAEL COLLINS' LIFE — SO FAR.

AS THIS IS WRITTEN IN 2016, HE'S STILL
GOING STRONG AT 86 YEARS OLD.

IT'S EASY TO GET LOST WHEN YOU'RE
THE GUY WHO STAYED WITH THE SHIP WHILE
ALDRIN AND ARMSTRONG WALKED ON THE
MOON. BUT AS COLLINS ALWAYS SAID,
APOLLO MISSIONS WERE DESIGNED FOR THREE
PEOPLE, AND EACH OF THEM WAS CRITICAL
TO THE MISSIONS' SUCCESS.

APOLLO 11 COULDN'T HAVE HAPPENED
WITHOUT HIM. HE WAS THE MAN WHO GOT
THEM THERE, AND GOT THEM HOME AGAIN.

A TIMELINE OF SPACE EXPLORATION

Advances in space exploration have been made over centuries with help from inventors all over the world. Here are some milestones:

Eleventh century: Chinese inventors create gunpowder, which will later be used to fuel the first rockets.

Seventeenth century: Hyder Ali, Sultan of Mysore, builds the first metal rocket.

March 16, 1926: Robert Goddard launches the first liquid-fueled rocket.

October 3, 1942: German engineers launch the first ballistic missile, the V-2.

September 1945: With the end of World War II, many German scientists are brought to the United States.

October 14, 1947: Chuck Yeager breaks the sound barrier in the X-1 test plane.

October 4, 1957: The Soviet Union launches *Sputnik,* the world's first satellite. The Space Race begins.

November 3, 1957: The Soviets launch *Sputnik 2,* carrying the first animal in space, a dog named Laika. She does not survive.

October 1, 1958: The National Aeronautics and Space Administration, or NASA, is created.

January 31, 1958: The United States launches its first satellite, *Explorer 1.*

January 2, 1959: The Soviets launch *Luna 1,* the first human-made object to leave Earth orbit.

August 7, 1959: NASA launches *Explorer 6,* which returns the first photographs of Earth taken from space.

April 12, 1961: Yuri Gagarin becomes the first human in space, aboard *Vostok 1.* He is also the first human to orbit the Earth.

May 5, 1961: Alan Shepard becomes the first American in space.

May 25, 1961: President John F. Kennedy challenges the nation to land an American on the moon before the end of the decade.

February 20, 1962: John Glenn is the first American to orbit the Earth.

June 16, 1963: Valentina Tereshkova becomes the first woman in space, piloting *Vostok 6.*

March 18, 1965: Cosmonaut Alexei Leonov makes the first spacewalk, from *Voshod 2.*

March 23, 1965. Virgil "Gus" Grissom becomes the first man to go to space twice, aboard *Gemini 3*.

February 3, 1966: The unmanned Soviet craft *Luna 9* makes the first controlled landing on the moon.

March 16, 1966: *Gemini 8* performs the first docking maneuver between two spacecraft

April 3, 1966: The Soviet *Luna 10* probe is the first spacecraft to orbit the moon

January 27, 1967: All three astronauts aboard *Apollo 1* die during a simulated launch.

April 23, 1967: Cosmonaut Vladimir Komarov dies aboard *Soyuz 1* when it crashes after re-entry.

July 20, 1969: *Apollo 11* lands on the moon.

November 13, 1971: *Mariner 9* is the first spacecraft to orbit Mars and map its surface.

January 5, 1972: President Richard Nixon announces development of the space shuttle, a reusable launch vehicle.

April 12, 1981: *Columbia* is the first space shuttle to launch and complete a mission.

June 18, 1983: Sally Ride becomes the first American woman in space, aboard the space shuttle *Challenger*.

January 28, 1986: The space shuttle *Challenger* explodes shortly after launch, killing all seven crew members.

July 4, 1997: *Pathfinder* and *Sojourner* land and begin exploring the surface of Mars.

November 20, 1998: The International Space Station is launched. (It remained in service as of 2016.)

February 1, 2003: The space shuttle *Columbia* disintegrates on re-entry, killing all seven crew members.

November 26, 2011: The *Curiosity* rover becomes the most recent Mars vehicle to make a successful landing. It remained operational as of 2016 and has detected evidence of liquid water, critical for human missions to Mars.

2030s: The target date for the first human mission to Mars.

FURTHER READING

Buzz Aldrin and Wendy Minor, *Look to the Stars*. Putnam, 2009. Starting with Isaac Newton, Aldrin and Minor give younger kids a tour of the history of spaceflight, moving all the way up to test pilots and pioneers of rocketry. And he doesn't stop there, envisioning what Martian colonies and space exploration might be like.

Andrew Chaikin, *Mission Control, This Is Apollo: The Story of the First Voyages to the Moon*. Viking, 2009. An illustrated large-format overview of the early space program, from the first Mercury capsules through the moon landings.

Michael Collins, *Carrying the Fire: An Astronaut's Journeys*. Farrar, Straus and Giroux, 2009. The subject of this book tells his own story.

Brian Floca, *Moonshot: The Flight of Apollo 11*. Atheneum, 2009. A picture book with poetic text, for younger children.

Dave Goldberg, *A User's Guide to the Universe*. Wiley, 2010. A funny and entertaining book about everything from the Big Bang to life on other planets.

Catherine Thimmesh, *Team Moon: How 400,000 People Landed Apollo 11 on the Moon*. Houghton Mifflin, 2006. The story of everyone but the astronauts, showing how it took literally hundreds of thousands of people—from seamstresses to computer programmers to machinists to engineers—to put three men on the moon.

ONLINE RESOURCES

NASA's Apollo 11 Mission Overview
https://www.nasa.gov/mission_pages/apollo/missions/apollo11.html. This is a great place to find out more about the Apollo 11 mission, with pictures and video as well as a detailed summary. It also has links to other resources, including transcripts of conversations between the astronauts and Mission Control.

The Smithsonian Air and Space Museum Apollo 11 page
https://airandspace.si.edu/events/apollo11/. The Apollo 11 capsule, scorched from re-entry, is on display inside the front door of the Air and Space Museum. Go see it if you can! But if you can't, this web site is a pretty good substitute.

The Lunar and Planetary Institute
http://www.lpi.usra.edu/lunar/missions/apollo/apollo_11/. The institute maintains a great collection of science-focused materials, including articles about the experiments the Apollo 11 astronauts performed, moon maps, and articles about further exploration of the solar system.

Tilbury House Publishers
12 Starr Street
Thomaston, Maine 04861
800-582-1899 · www.tilburyhouse.com

Text © 2017 by Alex Irvine
Illustrations © 2017 by Ben Bishop

Hardcover ISBN 978-088448-452-3
eBook ISBN 978-9-88448-537-7

First hardcover printing: March 2017

15 16 17 18 19 20 XXX 10 9 8 7 6 5 4 3 2 1

Library of Congress Control Number: 2016959437

Designed by Frame 25 Productions
Printed in Shenzhen, China, by Shenzhen Caimei Printing Co., Ltd.,
through Four Colour Print Group, Louisville, KY

ALEX IRVINE wanted to be an astronaut when he was a kid, but his first pair of glasses ended that dream. Instead he became a writer, with forty-odd books to his credit. He also writes games and comics. Other upcoming projects include *The Comic Book Story of Baseball*, an interactive novel called *Powers That Be*, and an as-yet-unnamed fantasy trilogy. Still a space nerd who cried the first time he saw the Apollo 11 capsule at the Smithsonian, he lives in South Portland, Maine, with his wife Lindsay, four children, two dogs, a bird, and a snake. You can find him on Twitter (@alexirvine) or Facebook.

BEN BISHOP is a comic creator from Portland Maine. He wrote, illustrated, and self-published his first book, a 300-page graphic novel called *Nathan the Caveman*, in 2008, and followed it with several other smaller works. In 2011 he provided the illustrations for the award-winning book *Lost Trail: Nine Days Alone in the Wilderness*, the graphic novel retelling of the famous Donn Fendler story *Lost on a Mountain in Maine*. He has done mainstream cover artwork for characters like the Teenage Mutant Ninja Turtles, Bebop and Rocksteady, Batman, Transformers and Gijoe. He is currently working on his next book, *The Aggregate*, a Split Decision graphic novel coming soon.